GOOD MOMENTS

Monsieur Wagner a de beaux moments,
mais de mauvais quart d'heures.

Gioacchino Rossini to Emile Naumann
April 1867

GOOD MOMENTS

A Publishing Retrospect

❧

FILLETED BY

MICHAEL RUSSELL

MICHAEL RUSSELL

First published in Great Britain 2002
by Michael Russell (Publishing) Ltd
Wilby Hall, Wilby, Norwich NR16 2JP

Typeset in Sabon by Waveney Typesetters
Wymondham, Norfolk
Printed and bound in Great Britain
by Biddles Ltd, Guildford and King's Lynn

Designed by Humphrey Stone

ISBN 0 85955 276 4

For my *arbiter elegantiae*
HUMPHREY STONE

Contents

CONTENTS

Introduction

❧

I like odd credentials. I've seen an Egyptian goose through a hole in a Digestive biscuit. I've also survived thirty years as a solo publisher. I don't know which is odder, but in *Good Moments* I've gone for the publishing. It's a distillation of a lot of effort without the accumulation of much prosperity, distance rather than growth, 'whew' rather than 'wow'. The catch is that if you finish last in the marathon you've still made the mistake of running as far as the others.

There are others of us around of course, two or three of them old friends, though most operate in more specific markets – regional or green or business and so on. There are plenty more in the commercial cemeteries who started off like us and for one reason or another got things wrong. Not that getting things right is much of a picnic. In my case it means supervising every single aspect of every book I produce, from drawing up the contract to sending out the review copies. Please don't tell me that's bad business. The parallel I put in the mouth of J. R. Hartley – that 'talking to me about business is rather like talking to Mowgli about the Seven Years War' – is beginning to look a little auto-descriptive

The selection is difficult. One or two birds have flown and the rights have reverted or moved on elsewhere – Paul Theroux's *Sailing through China*, for instance, or the little book I did with Paul Theroux and Bruce Chatwin, *Patagonia Revisited.* But first and foremost, some books can be filleted much more easily than others: you can isolate passages which may still interest or entertain without being swamped in an explanation of the context. So commercial success isn't necessarily a criterion either. The two books that sold the most copies in my editions, apart from Dean Sydney Evans's *Salisbury Cathedral: A Reflective Guide*, are neither of them represented – Tony Morrison's *Pathways to the Gods: The Mystery of the Andes*

Lines and the Duke of Edinburgh's *A Question of Balance* (the mystery there being why it was entrusted to me). There is also the question of space; there isn't room for even ten per cent of the list. So some categories that I've tackled in my disparate output aren't represented at all – religion amongst them. And if that makes you raise your eyes to heaven, it's appropriate but not part of the strategy.

I'd been floundering about for some while as a literary agent when I was asked to put together a reference book for an American publisher. It came out quite well, in content and appearance, and I decided to publish the UK edition myself. We lived then at Wilton, near Salisbury (we moved to our present address in 1991), and initially I joined forces with the Compton Press, a Wiltshire printer and occasional publisher, to start the imprint Compton Russell. It got away happily enough – it was there that Humphrey Stone and I began our long association and he has been my friend and *arbiter elegantiae* ever since. (The clocktower that he drew for my colophon surmounted the Compton Press machine room at Compton Chamberlayne.) But the publishing instincts were not really compatible and the Press and I parted company. They hit the buffers soon afterwards, victims I suppose of technological change but having done much to be proud of. There were some good characters who worked there, mostly craftsmen who were as congenial as some of their union masters at that time were professionally graceless. 'Pathfinder' wasn't a craftsman, though he was equally congenial. He was for a time the van driver and, early in his employment, returned with a full load having been unable to find London. He'd got to Staines, so he was getting warm. I believe he closed in later like a veteran.

I pressed on with my now eponymous wares. The first book for Michael Russell Publishing was Virginia Surtees's *A Beckford Inheritance: The Lady Lincoln Scandal* (abstracted here), and that pleases me particularly. We are very different creatures – her manners are much better than mine – but we're friends. We went on to do six more titles together, though that didn't land Virginia the Lady Authors' Output Cup. She was pipped by that archetypal outnumberer Freya

Stark with her eight volumes of Letters. But more of Dame Freya anon, because even she took second overall place to Bishop Michael Mann whose six military titles (seven if you include the Regimental history he wrote and I produced for his old regiment, the Queen's Dragoon Guards) were augmented by *Some Windsor Sermons* and, co-written with the Duke of Edinburgh, A *Windsor Correspondence* and *Survival or Extinction?* Michael's personal goodwill had such a benign effect on sales that I suggested to him fairly early on that he should become the publisher while I took over as Dean of Windsor; but nothing came of it.

My relationship with Freya Stark was harmonious, in that it was without discord. I don't flatter myself that it was more than a business friendship, but it was extended because the diamond in our care wasn't merely as big as the Ritz and revealing because the corpus of letters on which we drew illumined quite personal aspects of her long life. I knew her of course in her years of consolidation, and consolidation requires more wily talents than achievement. It was unkindly said of her that when she was in her nineties and, forgivably, a little misty in the identification of visitors, she recaptured complete lucidity on the arrival of the Queen Mother. It's true that Freya had on occasion stayed at the Castle of Mey, and she would show me handwritten letters from the Queen Mother approving our succeeding volumes. I don't think the Queen Mother was just being gracious with the crumbs of position; I could imagine them seeing the point of each other, fitting into each other's different landscape, Ossa and Pelion without the stacking. Freya may have liked people who were grand, but she also liked people who could glean from experience and talk about it. Yet for someone so generally perceptive she could on some things be puzzlingly ingenuous. I suspect the little girl act was secretly stage-managed. There is a story that her house in Asolo was designed in feet and built in metres; with Freya herself it seemed to be the other way round. In the blurb for Volume Two, I see I referred to her 'confident humility, such as small giants must feel in the presence of enormous dwarfs'. Today I'd have been prosecuted by the National Council for the Goliathly Challenged; at the time a reviewer (Paul Scott) said he wished he'd thought of it himself. And he knew her well enough for it to strike a chord.

It was a blessing to have Lucy Moorehead editing the Letters (and when she was tragically killed, her daughter Caroline). At first Freya would defend every phrase as if it were Hill 60, but gradually we became more trusted with our editorial suggestions. We always knew that the volume covering the marriage (Volume Six) might give us the most problems. There had presumably been some misapprehensions on the part of the bride (who was by then already rather into extra time – and her husband, to extend the sporting analogy, wasn't your conventional striker), and we felt there might be scores to settle; but in the event she was a model of good grace. Over the seventh volume, which covered Freya's following of Alexander's path in Asia Minor, there was considerable debate about possible titles. I mischievously suggested 'Some Talk of Alexander' (from 'The British Grenadiers') and Freya grabbed at it, apparently unconscious of the allusion and the shift in intonation.

It was not always such plain sailing. When I was publishing Sir Bernard Burrows's book on the Gulf in Transition, I asked him whether he had any preferences over a title. 'Footnotes in the Sand,' he said. I remember twirling around in the window seat in the room we used at Wilton for serious guests when it wasn't raining (a drip from the flat roof above the bay, landing in the wrong place, could come across as slightly sub-executive). 'You can't call it that,' I said, '"Footnotes in the Sand" by Bernard Burrows. It's one of those jokes. It's Eileen Dover.' He looked at me in total incomprehension. I didn't try to explain, my *gravitas* ratings were already in free fall. 'Footnotes in the Sand' it was. And nobody laughed. Well, I did, a bit.

The supply lines of publishable material have always been an anxiety. Unsolicited manuscripts are in the main bad news, simply because they are almost always unpublishable (especially when you're near the bottom of the barrel) and because they take up time. Being a solo publisher may be healthy for the overheads but you have to face up to frequent personal chores. And acknowledging and returning a load of rubbish is a grade A chore. It so happens that I respect any author's pain of gestation and I haven't the heart to be too dismissive, because I know that writing a rotten book is likely to be just as much lonely effort as writing a good one. However, I don't want an argument about it, so I was nettled when a man disputed my opinion of his opus. I had to tell him, which I hadn't been going to divulge, that his chances of finding a publisher were significantly poorer than my chances of becoming Mayor of Beirut. Perhaps he was researching my Near Eastern connections, but he didn't reply. There was then an embarrassing shift of moral supremacy when a third of the first page of his typescript was eaten by a slug. I'm a bit of a floor filer (it wasn't just that his typescript was finding its proper level) and during the night the slug broke through a gap in the skirting board and started tucking into chapter one. It obviously liked the material more than I had because it returned on successive nights – although the typescript, less page one, was by now in the post. We eventually saw the midnight feaster. It was huge, anaemic-looking, and repulsive. The dog ran away from it. We christened it Slurpico and it left a broad wake on the carpet like a liner. When it had made its way back via the skirting board and out through a drain into a flower bed for the hours of daylight, we made good the defences. I offered no explanation for the missing page.

I seem to have done my fair share of books about India. The first was Bill Saumarez Smith's *A Young Man's Country* (Paul Scott's phrase), which described the life of a subdivisional officer in the Indian Civil Service in 1936–37. There's always something of a tug of war between the arguments against imperialism and the evidence of the integrity of so many of its servants. The intelligent fair-mindedness of *A Young Man's Country* was a reminder of that. The author's son John, an old friend and the unshuddering tiller of Heywood Hill's bookshop in London W1, has always been an invaluable source of advice and a most effective champion of many of my books. Heywood Hill and John Sandoe, one step south in SW3, are perhaps my most enduring supporters. If that says something about them as well as about my list, it's apparently something none of us mind: it's a sunny relationship.

To return to India. Zoë Yalland's two books about the British in Cawnpore – *Traders and Nabobs* (1765–1857) and its successor *Boxwallahs* (1857–1901) – were of particular value because they were about the commercial classes. It's the official classes who tend to write imperial history, whereas the commercial classes very often have something quite as interesting to say about the development of a community. Zoë had been born in India and ran a school there for a while. The compilation of the two books was an extended affair and I got to know her well. When *Boxwallahs* was nearly ready to go, she was told she was dying of cancer. It was a time-consuming production, with well over 500 pages and 160 integrated illustrations, and quite a bit of editorial input. Then when we had page proofs a burglar removed the typesetter's computer, including Zoë's back up discs. I remember two consecutive eighteen-hour days of scanning, reading and re-proofing. By the time the book was printed and delivered to the bindery, it was evident that time was running short, so I had an advance copy specially bound and took it to her in the Norwich hospice. It really seemed to give her brief remission. To have lost that particular race would have been painful. Her daughter had been married to Andrew Motion (and retained that surname into her second marriage – a nice slant on perpetual Motion) and our Laureate-to-be published a poem in memory of Zoë in the *Times Literary Supplement*, affectionately meant, I'm sure, but with a whiff of bleakness about it which made some of us uneasy.

Richard Terrell did three books about India, the first of which, *The Chief Justice*, about his father, is abstracted here. He then got an Arts Council grant for a visit to India which resulted in *A Perception of India*, and the third book was a collection of letters from the Indian Mutiny. He did two other books – one on his wartime experiences in West Africa – *West African Interlude* – and a good, but neglected, childhood memoir, *Still Life with Voices*. Like his father, he liked to make walking expeditions and arrived more than once at our house in Wilton, dressed in rather short shorts and wearing a beret, to consult us about local routes and resting places.

Sir Owain Jenkins's *Merchant Prince* was an accomplished

account of life in India that extended into commercial life after Independence. He came to me at the instigation of Philip Mason, an old India hand and a natural stylist if ever there was one. Philip and I did several things together. Apart from the *Merchant Prince* connection, he edited and urged on me two books which were very well received: Pamela Scott's memoir of Kenya, *A Nice Place to Live*, and the idiosyncratic and often very funny Irish memoir by Kevin FitzGerald, *With O'Leary in the Grave*. It would have been a natural for these pages. It went into paperback with Oxford University Press, the author died and I didn't pursue the question of the present copyright ownership. However, what has been a surprise is that Philip Mason's own second volume of autobiography, *A Thread of Silk*, somehow doesn't work for abstraction. It is predominantly about his experience over here with the Race Relations Board, and – to me at any rate – it just doesn't wear well. Philip, who lived not far from us when we were in Wiltshire, had the frustrating experience of making a reputation for himself under a pseudonym before writing successfully under his own name. It was as Philip Woodruff that he wrote, for instance, his classic *The Men Who Ruled India*. He was amused when I told him that one of the anecdotes in it concerned my grandfather (yes, grandfather) who as a young man at the time of the Mutiny shielded his magistrate from a dissident sepoy who was taking aim at him with a rifle. For keeping that particular magistracy out of the sits. vac. my grandfather was awarded the Indian Mutiny Medal, and he does seem to have been a man of extraordinary nerve. He bullied the Indians for a while, then he was sent by Gladstone to bully the Irish. Late in life, and with his wife refusing to divorce him, he set up home with my grandmother and had three boys – my father and two uncles – and brought them up in strict Edwardian convention under an adopted identity. He had no choice but to maintain his metropolitan persona as Sir Edward Jenkinson (I see from surviving letters that he was painted by Hubert von Herkomer for the Daimler Company boardroom) and he returned to domestic life in Bedfordshire as Mr George Russell. His children never knew of this duplicity until they were almost coming of age and their father had died. And I think they were put out.

George Pottinger added to the Indian portfolio with *Mayo: Disraeli's Viceroy*. George wrote well, and we did two further books together – the rather arcane *The Real Admirable Crichton* and a book he co-authored with Sir Patrick Macrory, *The Ten-Rupee Jezail*, about the British retreat from Kabul in the First Afghan War. (An earlier Macrory book about the incident, *Signal Catastrophe*, had to be retitled in paperback because people thought it was about railways.) George was a bright man. He had been a very senior civil servant in Scotland but fell foul of the law over the matter of inducements and was sent to prison. One of the inducements was an account with a well-known tailor in Savile Row. As prosecuting counsel observed at his trial: 'Some achieve greatcoats; some have greatcoats thrust upon them.'

To complete the subcontinental round-up: Priscilla Napier did two volumes on Sir Charles Napier in India, *I Have Sind* and *Raven Castle*, more supportive of his reputation than Mayor Livingstone who has banned his statue from Trafalgar Square; and most recently I published Philip Glazebrook's *The Electric Rock Garden,* also abstracted here.

I never tried to write myself. I sometimes felt I ought to try but I knew I'd be too tortured about it. Anyway, having saddled myself with the labours of publishing, I could pretend now that I had no time. I'd done the odd literary competition: my extremely meagre supply of premium bonds were all acquired from winnings from the *New Statesman*. Reprovingly, they've never paid a dividend. I also won a Humorous Story Competition in *The Times* with a strange, rather surreal story called 'Tea with Mr Starling'. It was about a man in a Russian labour camp winning a chess competition where the prize was tea with Stalin, and it was, I must admit, quite dark. But does dark rule out humorous? The best humorous story, after all, isn't necessarily the one with the most jokes, any more than the best detective story is the one with the most detectives. Anyway, publication of the story was followed by indignant correspondence, one letter to *The Times* reporting that a poll had been taken on a Brighton commuter train which broadly agreed that the story was intrinsically not funny. That was deflating – people on a Brighton commuter train were likely to be expert on what wasn't funny. So it was a hollow moment, even if my effort had beaten – I was told – nearly a couple of thousand other entries and Tom Stoppard, no less, was one of the judges.

There'd been other complications too. Because I'd had publishing dealings with two people on *The Times* who were involved in the administration of the competition, I had entered, at random, in the name of our children's nanny's mother. She was an unemotional woman who lived locally and sometimes helped us in the house, unflustered that our younger boy was always jumping out on her and blowing a bicycle pump into her forward areas. Scores of times I heard her assess the human condition with a cryptic 'You don't know the half of it', but in the matter of the *Times* Humorous Story Competition there were two major knowledge dollops which were eluding her completely: a) that she was imminently going to be announced the winner of the £500 prize and b) that we needed the money for her daughter's wages. So I came clean with *The Times* about my identity and took the rap from the Brighton commuters.

This humourless humour problem came up again when I was commissioned by my friend Roddy Bloomfield to write *Fly Fishing by J. R. Hartley.* At the height of the Yellow Pages television campaign, almost everyone knew about the man in the advertisement trying to get hold of a second hand copy of his book. The unwritten *Fly Fishing*, Roddy reckoned, was the second best known book after the Bible. So I buckled down and wrote it – pretty quickly. And if that wasn't a tribute to Roddy's skills as an editorial persuader, I don't know what was. We did have some very enthusiastic reviews, but some sour ones as well. Because it was so well handled by Roddy and the battalions at Random House and because of the whole Yellow Pages involvement, it rose to the top of the best seller list: so the joke, if not in everyone's opinion by me, was at least with me. (It still sells, over ten years later, in Japanese translation – I think probably in the cookery departments of Japanese bookshops – and, to rub in the Yellow Pages joke, also modestly in China.) I even came across a reference to it in an earnest book on post-modernism. And, more important, there were a few people whose opinion I really minded about who genuinely liked it. So I'll settle for that. We went on to do *J. R. Hartley Casts Again* and then, after Roddy moved to Hodder, *Golfing by J. R. Hartley*. We're not confusing it with literary triumph, but in publishing terms the Hartley spoof was certainly a success. But then Roddy Bloomfield knows all about publishing success. Anyone who has had author dealings with him knows he's a star.

The J. R. Hartley experience threw up an instance of the occasional absurdity of public perception. According to the *Sunday Mercury* of 5 January 1992, people in the streets in Birmingham were asked what they knew, on the occasion of the hundredth anniversary of his birthday, about J. R. R. Tolkien, a son of the city. I quote the paper.

> Tolkien grew up in Birmingham and a plaque in his honour hangs outside Duchess Place in Edgbaston, near where his family lived in the early part of this century.
>
> Experts believe some of his most famous writings were inspired by the city.
>
> So the *Sunday Mercury* asked Birmingham workers and shoppers if they knew why Tolkien was famous …
>
> A quarter thought he was J. R. Hartley and more than half didn't have a clue who he was.
>
> The survey results caused dismay among members of the Tolkien Society.

As well they might.

I would get the odd 'honourable reject' from the bigger publishers which needed editorial attention and I had edited a few books for Roddy Bloomfield. One becomes a sort of literary chameleon adapting to an author's overall style. You don't need to be in George Eliot mode when you're fine-tuning Lester Piggott. But the mending has to be invisible. I've never had to edit fiction, and that must be extremely skilful. It's perfectly possible for someone who can't write commercially to improve the text of someone who can; but you notice that the editor tends to stay the editor, while the author continues to pick up the cheques. The gift is the narrative thrust, the whatever it is that keeps people turning the pages. That's what publishers pay for.

In appraising a typescript you get used to warning signs. The overuse of adjectives is a familiar blight. 'Great' is the worst. I coined a condition called 'greatitis' and you'd be amazed how many people suffer from it. I had one accomplished author who produced the word 'great' four times in one shortish paragraph. He was appalled when I pointed it out. What's most subversive about 'great' is that it's so often the *mot juste*. There are other adjectives, too, which send me signals. 'Splendid' can sometimes tell you more about the author than what he's writing about. If you come across 'splendid little man', remove the lid of the dustbin.

In my sort of rather suspect authorship there are temptations to self-indulgence. I remember I swapped with Nicholas Elliott his joke about the cricket-mad bishop wondering if the aisle would take spin, which I used in *Fly Fishing*, with a family joke of ours about a fashionable hairdresser we called Tintoregretto, which Nicholas used in *Never Judge a Man by His Umbrella*. And there were some jokes that got away. Trimming as usual, because organised shooting has always upset me, I agreed to cast an editorial eye over the text of Jonathan Ruffer's *The Big Shots: Edwardian Shooting Parties*, which (published by Debrett) had quite a success at the end of the 1970s. The picture research was not within my brief, and certainly Jonathan's gallery of often preposterous photographs contributed significantly to the book's appeal. I had one regret. There was a passage recounting that when King George V shot at Sandringham he had as his loader an estate employee who was almost identical in appearance. He grew his beard in the same style as the King 'and, whenever they appeared together, they always wore exactly the same clothing. It amused the King to see his guests unsure of whether they were talking to their monarch or an estate worker.' Sadly, no one turned up with a photograph of the dissembling duo. It begged for the caption 'Am I my keeper's brother?'

Along the way there were heroes. Terry Farmiloe, for instance, Terry the Typesetter, a loyal, good friend, robust in personal assessments and doyen of the typographical surprise. His health and his domestic life had both seen better days, although he was uncomplaining about either, and over one Christmas, to my lasting sadness, he fell gravely ill and died. We all said goodbye in the Poole crematorium with Abide with Me. Perhaps it should have been Abide with Em (and, dare I say it, might have been had Terry set the service sheet) – the Typesetter's Farewell, a felicitous literal if you know your printer's measures. I miss Terry. He once stayed all night in the office (where he was employee not proprietor) as we battled with an index against a morning deadline. That sort of precarious shared experience is the bond of bonds.

(On the subject of literals I can't resist dragging in something which unnerved and amused me at the time and which I confided to the readership of *The Times*: 'It's a bad moment for a publisher', I wrote, 'when, as has happened to me, an author writes to say he's checking his proofs for "littorals". What should be the definitive example of the genre? The Wilder Shores of Hove?')

The printing industry is probably unsurpassed in the area of inventive catastrophe. I thought I'd seen it all, but recently, with a tight schedule to meet, the fork-lift driver at the bindery split the pallet carrying the load of printed sheets and scattered them in the yard. So to the long litany of things that can go wrong I could add 'cleft pallet'. You mustn't let it worry you. I keep as my model a printing executive in whose office I was once standing while he was getting severe flak over the telephone from a customer. When it was all over he turned to me with a smile and said 'It's all water over my head.' I liked the phlegm and I loved the phraseology.

This mustn't descend into an acceptance speech, but it would be churlish not to thank 'Fitz' Fitzsimons and Rodney Ellis who have sold my books for ages and who know my rather maverick ways. It doesn't get any easier for a small publisher to get his stock into the bookshops and the rep may be a threatened species. For the sort of books I publish Fitz, in London, has the readier market, but it helps that people like him so much. We've all three covered a long road together.

We live ungrandly in a fine but spooky-looking house, with a formal garden in the front where some elementary geometry has been imposed on nature. I was dismissed as topiary officer by the co-director for turning something that should have looked like a pineapple into a gruyère, and my participation now is non-involved enjoyment: which is right because as a gardener I'd just make slow mistakes. The co-director is capable of a quick mistake but her long-term judgement seems extremely sound. There are slightly too many outbuildings, which we're not allowed to blow up – though, funnily enough, we could blow up the office and the warehouse, and sometimes think of it. It started life as a dairy, before our time. One scheduled barn we make available to two of our neighbours and friends. One used to have a top photographic retouching studio in London before the days of computer enhancement and now uses the barn for some incredibly skilled marine construction. He once spent five hours doctoring Nancy Reagan's wrinkles out of some photographs taken of her by Norman Parkinson. He helps with all my illustration sections and advises me on matters photographic. Like Humphrey Stone and me, he's neurotic about detail. Our other inmate used to work in a zoo and now does animal sculpture. He is probably the only person I know who has chauffeured a sedated lion through Dudley and Tipton, and certainly the only person I know who has chauffeured a sedated lion through Dudley and Tipton that unexpectedly came round.

It takes me less than half a minute nowadays to commute from the breakfast table to the office – perhaps a second or two more if the Norfolk bacon-slicer wind is blowing from the north – and I work productively for an hour or so until the telephone begins to interrupt. It asks for Customer Services or Accounts or the Stationery Buyer and I reply politely 'I can help.' The office is occasionally tidy, usually not; the packing room and the warehouse always not. About lunchtime, Brian the postman leaves the mail on the floor just inside the door, with a dog biscuit secured under the rubber band which Messerschmitt, our porridge-coloured dachsund, extracts with a little ping. In the afternoon the carriers' driver calls to pick up the parcels, sometimes with a huge biscuit to stop Messerschmitt barking at him, and stays briefly to talk – in the winter about football, in the summer about football with a dusting of cricket.

In publishing terms I know I'm largely out of touch, but I seem to keep in touch all right with that part of the book-buying market which is also out of touch. And anyway I like the whole gestation of the book, editorial and production, and I suppose I like it most if someone arrives as author and remains as friend. If there's a plus about solo publishing, it's that your books look all of a piece. The content and the look of the book should be harmonious. You can sometimes lose that when the book is passed from one department to another. I detect it sometimes with the bigger publishers, though the last thing they want is advice from me.

In my market, too, I tend to use better quality paper. People notice it (possibly because most publishers don't reckon it matters) and with short run publishing like mine I think it's money well spent. So I supply the printer with my own stock from the paper merchant rather than use his standard lines. With Humphrey Stone at my long-distance elbow, we mind, too, about type sizes and margins and leading and old-style figures and letter-spaced small capitals and all the rest of it – things that individually perhaps the public don't hoist in but which cumulatively have a style about them. And the cost of producing a decently laid out book is more or less the same as producing something that looks a mess. Sometimes we indulge in a typographic joke – I don't know why, because the only thing that's really funny about typographic jokes is that absolutely nobody sees them. But it's a good feeling when the books arrive from the bindery, you take out a copy and think, yes, that's right. It doesn't happen every time.

The auditors steer us annually through our two sets of accounts, for our close formation team of limited company and partnership; and remind me – not that I need reminding – to stick to what I can manage and not get trapped into overheads which would get me chasing turnover – the beginning of the end. Meanwhile the file copies edge along the bookshelves in increasing number, witness to countless hours of concentrated preparation. It's rather like when slowly ascending a high hill, you pause sometimes to survey the view and see a steady accretion of the landscape that almost compensates you for the effort of the climb. So that's my publishing. I wouldn't prescribe it, but I'm glad to have done it. No, I'm glad to be doing it.

Messerschmitt

The just managing director

The co-director with her football team in our Wiltshire days. The Burnbake Trust ran workshops for ex-young offenders, the Wilton workshop steered by the co-director. The team briefly topped the unHimalayan peak of the Salisbury Sunday League Division Three. Persimmon sponsored them. Thank you Mr Davidson.

Domestic headquarters

Publishing headquarters

Dear Animated Bust

LETTERS TO LADY JULIET DUFF

FRANCE 1915-1918

Maurice Baring

Primrose yellow background, white panel, black lettering

Maurice Baring

DEAR ANIMATED BUST: LETTERS TO LADY JULIET DUFF FRANCE 1915–1918

❧

Maurice Baring's incongruous success as an RFC staff officer is one of the First World War's few agreeable practical jokes. In all probability he saw these letters as a lifeline, a civilising distraction from the mental and physical discomforts of the war, written to someone who may have missed a good deal of the subtleties but at least fostered the flow. The letters were typeset at the end of the war, incorporating – almost to the point of annoyance – the idiosyncrasies of their original typewritten form. Three sets of galley proofs survived (all very unevenly inked) – one for Juliet Duff, one for Maurice Baring and one for Hilaire Belloc; and there the project rested. Baring drew on the letters, in edited form, for his 'Flying Corps Headquarters 1914–1918', without referring at all to Lady Juliet. I reproduced a truncated version from one of the original sets of galleys, taking a chance that the quirkiness of presentation wouldn't irritate the reader.

These Baring letters are quite a contrast to his friend Raymond Asquith's tour de force offerings from the Western Front (I published 'Raymond Asquith: Life and Letters', edited by John Jolliffe, in my Clocktower paperback series). There is a slightly caustic detachment about Asquith which sometimes coruscates more than it endears. Maurice Baring, on the other hand, even in the comparatively disorderly writing of 'Dear Animated Bust', disposes you to like him. His writing smiles.

Because she had just completed a biography of her grandfather, Aubrey Herbert, entitled 'The Man Who Was Greenmantle', which had taken her very much into Maurice Baring's world, I asked Margaret FitzHerbert (Evelyn Waugh's second daughter) to write an introduction to 'Dear Animated Bust'. Here it is.

Maurice Baring was already forty when the First World War began. He did not belong to that endlessly extolled, doomed, 'golden' generation, nor yet to the generation of their parents. He was neither 'soul' nor 'slip', but fell between the two and mixed naturally with both, a ubiquitous and cherished figure in the memoirs of the period. Born in 1874, the eighth of ten children of the first Lord Revelstoke, he was brought up in a privileged, talented, highly educated circle. His childhood was cloudlessly happy: his jokes and culture were rooted in those days of fräulein and mademoiselle and teasing brothers and sisters, and something of that youthful simplicity and humour never left him. He remained unmarried, and at the end of his life, by then a victim of Parkinson's Disease, went to live with Lady Lovat and her children at Beaufort Castle in Inverness-shire. He died in 1945.

His literary reputation flourished after the First World War, although his popularity as a novelist was always greater in France than in England. He was a distinguished translator of Russian, French, German and Italian, and a perceptive critic of literature, drama and music. He had not, however, been originally directed towards a life of letters. After Eton and Cambridge, he had been put down for the Diplomatic Service, to which he seemed admirably suited. But his entrance into this career was long delayed by an inability to pass simple examinations in geography and arithmetic. In 1898 two terms spent unofficially at Oxford brought him into contact with a younger Balliol fellowship which gathered round his two most intimate Oxford friends, Bron Herbert (later Lord Lucas) and Raymond Asquith; while Hilaire Belloc, Baring's senior by four years, became also a close friend. Baring's conversion to Roman Catholicism in 1909 brought him still closer to Belloc. They wrote to each other regularly over the years, frequently in verse:

Dear Maurice,
You write better than Horace;
For you at your worst write madly,
Whereas he at his worst wrote badly.
But neither of us
Writes as well as Theocritus.

Baring joined up in the first few days of the war. Although he had no military training or background, he happened to be a friend of Sir David Henderson, Director of Military Training at the War Office. Henderson was put in charge of the newly formed Royal Flying Corps and agreed to take on Baring as an intelligence officer. The result was that Baring arrived out in France on 12 August 1914, ahead of most of the Regular Army and ahead of all the amateurs. While Henderson was in command, Baring's job was safe and he soon made himself indispensable. He mastered not only the jargon of aviation, which he was able to translate into French, but he actually understood the use and value of each nut and bolt.

When Henderson returned to London and Trenchard took over the command of the Royal Flying Corps in France, the outlook changed. Trenchard already knew Baring from an earlier visit to France. Baring had been delegated to meet Trenchard and get him to Headquarters, but the old problem with geography caused them to strike north from Boulogne, instead of east to St Omer. 'A certain intuition', Baring wrote in 'Flying Corps Headquarters 1914–1918', 'warned me after a time that we were going the wrong way.' Trenchard, when he arrived to take command in August 1915, had not forgotten the incident and intended to sack Baring, whose unmilitary manner and artistic tastes did nothing to dispel Trenchard's prejudice. He was put on one month's probation. 'I felt adrift, like a stranded bondsman face to face with a new Pharaoh, and a bondsman who felt he had no qualifications.' Happily, in the end, Trenchard kept him on and later wrote that Baring 'was almost my second sight in all the difficult tasks that came ... He knew more about what really mattered in war – how to deal with human nature, how to stir up those who wanted stirring, how to damp down those who were too excitable, how to encourage those who were in need of it – than any man I ever knew.'

Baring's correspondence with Lady Juliet Duff thus flowered in the interstices of a busy, difficult and sometimes dangerous life at the Front. She was not an obviously appropriate recipient for epistolary fireworks. Neither an intellectual nor a Catholic, she was not even clever or well-educated, although she hid her ignorance quite amiably behind a wall of vagueness. It was just as well that Baring affected a profound dislike for clever women. Nor was she accounted much of a beauty by her contemporaries, though both Baring and Belloc thought her lovely. Her gift was that of sympathy; she was a good listener.

Born in 1881, she was the only child of the fourth Earl of Lonsdale. She married Sir Robin Duff in 1903. He was killed in action in October 1914. In 1919 she married Major Keith Trevor, but the marriage ended in divorce in 1926. A rhyme from Maurice Baring survives:

> I've written plenty enough
> To Juliet Duff;
> I'll write nothing whatever
> To Juliet Trevor.

And a random selection from the letters themselves.

7.4.16
Bonnie sweet Bessie,

I send you my best wishes and my kind regards. General Rawlinson is wearing black field boots. On the other hand General Birch is wearing buff or beige puttees. General Trenchard is wearing brown field boots. Captain Baring is wearing gaiters.

Ever your most obedient
Lausbube

22.4.16
Dear Sir,

Very many thanks for yours of yesterday. With regard to the request made by you and recently reiterated that I should forward you a cheque for the amount due to you, I have to remind you that bright gold is not the thing that is most rare in the sad-hoped life of mortals nor do steel nor couches of silver nor the heavy-laden fields, fruitful in themselves, of the spacious earth so shine to the eye as the single-minded spirit of good men.

Never therefore be tempted to barter virtue for unjust gain. The best thing for a mortal is to have health, and the next to have been born fair of form, and the third to be rich without guile, and the fourth to have fun with your friends.

It is regrettable, Sir, that none of these conditions are fulfilled in your case.

My last word therefore shall be that virtue has sure glory, but wealth is sometimes an apanage of the basest among men. Please lay all this to heart and don't bother me further with your so-called account. Remember that war is war and that necessity knows no law. Recall to mind the pregnant phrase of the German Minister with regard to a scrap of paper and never forget that it behoves us to be economical in paper as well as in red gold or notes of currency.

I am Sir, with great truth,
Your obedient Servant
(for) M. Diagoras
W. T. Le Phill

Messrs Moulton & Co,
Furniture Dealers,
Great Portland Street,
London

11.9.16
Dear Bella Donna,

The news is that an Army Order is about to be published

according to which in future the shaving of the Upper Lip will be optional but the Knut or Toothbrush moustache will no longer be tolerated. This seals the doom of Bron's moustache. I must write and tell him today. I wonder what the Germans will think of this and what their countermove will be. They may possibly sack Hindenburg.

I wrote 20 letters yesterday, mostly to shops.

Shops are I find the best correspondents although they are sparing of news.

Yrs A. Men

20.5.17
Songe frivole,

We are awaiting the arrival of Colonel Grant who has not yet come. I am suffering from a dearth of summer socks, not too thick. Please order me some at Turnbull and Assers, Jermyn Street. They have my size. Or should have. If they haven't, tell them my foot is the same size as that of the Achilles statue in Hyde Park.

Have you read Wells' book about the Finite God? He believes in three Gods but not in one person. One is veiled, one is a kind of ferret and the other is an immortal friend who is doing his best in a hopeless situation like Prometheus Bound. It is a schoolboyish book. Halfbaked and cela ne tient pas debout. But it his expression of a religious experience: mixed with his ancient rebellion against Exeter Hall which is the only form of Christianity he has come across and which overshadowed his childhood or boyhood or both.

The book will probably annoy the NoGoddites. It will make Catholics smile. Wells knows no history save that of the cheaper books of reference and the Encyclopaedia Britannica.

Yours hopeful
The Man who was

26.5.17
Lampe joyeuse,

The socks are perfect, both as to texture, shade, colour and weight. The ties are exquisite and match the colour of the war landscape without attracting the attention of hostile aircraft. So they want an English motto for Tanks. Diable. English is an analytic and not a synthetic language. Have they thought of that? Have they realised that what you can say in one word in Latin takes twelve words to say in English?

I can think of nothing except Die Hard or Last Ditch. Or Thorough or la fumée passe le tank reste. Which God knows is true. Hillary [Belloc] arrives this afternoon from Paris. I want you to impress upon him that it was a wonderful thing and an act of great friendliness on the part of the General to send a car to Paris to meet and fetch him and have him here to stay: vu many things: one that he is very busy, very tired, very much harassed, and obliged to cope with a stream of unbidden guests including Joynson Hicks M.P.

The weather is gorgeous. It is like it used to be before the war when men and women went to Ascot and sat out in gardens in the middle of the night while others danced in ballrooms. Do you remember those days? ...

I have had two cheerful letters from the Russian Army, both from officers. Both say that perfect order reigns in their ranks.

Let us hope this is so.

Je vous salue,

Yours always
Paul de Musset

4.7.17
Enfant de Cypris,

A Russian pilot came here called Nolken. He had a happy day at the Depot. He was very nice.

I have been made a Major. I am sorry to part with the title of Captain. A Captain as you know combines the fire of the subaltern with the discretion of the field officer. I say goodbye to the fire of the subaltern.

I am sorry Beerbohm Tree is dead.

I have read Bourget's latest book. It is a good story spun out with rather tiresome comments. His books would be excellent if they were written by someone else.

Ne forçons point notre talent.

I remain your affectionate Major
Baring

29.8.17

Seraphim du Soir,

The gale has somewhat abated but the squalls continue to drift in from nowhere. Captain Acton RN arrived here last night a self-invited guest. He had a toothache and was peevish at the thought of nearly having to sleep in a hut. This was averted however, so all was well.

Yesterday we went to present Guillemer with his DSO. He was covered with medals from head to breast – French, Russian, Belgian, Serbian, Montenegran, Italian. But no German nor Austrian. He is very nice but looks very ill and white.

I gave him your best love and he said he remembered meeting you years ago in the Bois de Boulogne. I said that no doubt you remembered it too and that at any rate if you did you would certainly take pains not to forget it. Then he looked pensive and said 'Est elle toujours aussi belle?' I sighed and said you were more beautiful than ever. Then we both sighed.

Then we had tea. Tomorrow Lord Cowdray arrives ... [*later, 31.8.17*] He is the Head of the Air Board but only the mention of anything connected with the air suffocates him with boredom. He is a kind old man but no longer in his prime. We are a funny nation to do these things in war time.

Your long suffering
De la Rue

11.12.17

O Amabel,

So Jerusalem has been taken again after an interval of 733 years but Hillary says the Christians lost it in July and the Times says October. This is the way historians disagree. Please ask him whether he is right or wrong. It was very tactful of General Allenby not to shell it and I expect he will refrain from all theatrical antics in the manner of his entry.

So as to contrast with the behaviour of the German Emperor.

The weather is again raw and far from pleasant.

So I will draw to a close and subscribe myself your faithful
Geoffrey de Bouillon

12.12.17

Blest single siren,

I have just come in after an extensive tour. Nobody appears to have wooden undercarriages in the RE8 yet which is perplexing. I have a great longing to go to Jerusalem now that it belongs to General Allenby. But I suppose that you would rather go to great Seleucia built by Grecian Kings or where the sons of Eden long before dwelt in Telassar.

Yours with the kindest regards,
Jacques Tournebroche

27.12.17

Queen of the stars so gentle so benign,

Christmas is over. We had tepid turkey and cold bread sauce and flat champagne and port made of furniture polish. After dinner there was a concert. The electric lighting was wonderful, as it would be managed by mechanics and the best electricians in the world. It was better than Reinhardt or the Moscow Art Theatre or Gordon Craig.

A strong man gave an exhibition of strength.

But the assistants who had ill rehearsed their parts nearly killed him by stamping on the wrong portions of his body when he was trying to lift up a dumbbell weighing 200 lbs.

The ground is deep with snow. We intend to come to England for some days in a day or so.

I wish you the compliments of the season and remain

Yours unsolaced,
Thomas Clarkson

30.7.18
Dear Madame Patey,

Asprey is being very tiresome about my watch but I fear there is nothing to be done. C'est la guerre. But if you pass that way you might prod him with a parasol and say 'Please Mr Asprey get a move on with the Major's watch.'

Did you hear the story of Sir Douglas [Haig] saying to a private soldier 'Well my man, when did you start the war?'

'Who says I started the war?' answered the man.

Your remote
Scented Kendal Brown

And finally a selection of the distinctly unconventional forms of address and signatures from some of the letters. Some of them will have meant as little to Juliet Duff as the snippets about epicyclic gearing and the Acland deflector which the author pleasingly interpolates into the correspondence.

Chère arc-en-ciel nué de cent sortes de soies ...
Yrs sincerely
Kuli Khan (Nawab) Abbas
Recreations Stargazing

Torch-bearing Daughter of Night the dark Bosomed ...
Yours surely
De Horsey (Admiral)

Adorable Place Pigalle ...
Yours still
Waters run deep

Dark veiled Cotytto ...
Your in some respects
star-led wizard
Cyriack Skinner

Sweet Queen of Parley, daughter of the Illustrated London News (the above literary allusion will not be detected by you unless you invoke the aid of a scholar, I suggest E Marsh) ...

I remain
Your
Tantae pulchritudinis amator,
Pithy Ass

Chère Plusqueparfaite ...
Yours
Passé Défini

Linda zagaleja ...
Yours with kind regards
H.J.Ryman Ltd

Wilfrid Blunt

MARRIED TO A SINGLE LIFE
AN AUTOBIOGRAPHY
1901–1938

❧

I look now at the reviews for 'Married to a Single Life' (1983) and find them glowing: 'very warmly recommended' (Marghanita Laski in 'Country Life'); 'a delightful and beautifully written first volume of autobiography' ('Sunday Times'); 'a touching and enchanting book' ('The Observer'). But the privations and bizarre personnel of the public school life of Wilfrid's day, whether as pupil or master, rather lose their glow with the passage of time, well captured though they are. Without the camaraderie that went with it, spartan philistinism begins to look very like spartan philistinism. Re-reading the book, I find that some of it doesn't entertain me as much as it did, though it is full of good touches. Certainly the homosexual theme is most sensitively covered, in particular Wilfrid's physically unconsummated affection for Stephen Haggard. Wilfrid was a stylish, amusing writer, good company, with a couple of dozen other books to his credit – among which 'The Art of Botanical Illustration' (1950) was a seminal work.

This is unashamedly schoolboy chestnut humour; but try not to be at least slightly amused.

Yes, I liked boys. I liked their freshness, their vivacity, their candour. I liked their unexpected and engaging absurdity. I liked their credulity: my joking suggestion that two brothers in the school called Darewski must obviously be the sons of Paderewski was instantly accepted as fact. I liked the kind of naiveté that let one of them innocently conclude an essay on Canada, 'And so we come to the other end of England's largest daughter'. How, I was once asked in all seriousness, did one set about getting an artistic licence? ... Another, set an essay on 'Riddles', gave as an example one which he must have overheard but whose meaning had obviously escaped him: 'What is the animal that has twenty-two legs but only one ball?' – answer, 'A ladies' hockey eleven'. Yet more curious was a reply to the question, 'What is bottomry?' – '... another word for ... arson'; and it is said to have come as something of a surprise to one of the chaplains that St Martin shared his cloak with a bugger.

John Talbot was headmaster at Haileybury when Wilfrid joined the staff in 1923.

Routine had become distasteful to him, the dispatch of business irksome. Appointments to his staff – perhaps the most important part of a headmaster's duty – were usually made in haste and not infrequently repented. But these defects were, in part at any rate, offset by his genius for handling people. Parents who had come several hundred miles to see him by appointment might find he had gone off to Kew to look at rock plants; but if they were fortunate enough to catch him, they fell instant victims to his charm. A North-Country businessman came south in a rage to sue the school for the alleged wrongful dismissal of his son. An hour later he was writing Talbot a cheque for a hundred pounds as a contribution to the new Science Schools.

If dealing with people was Talbot's greatest natural gift, gardening was at this time his greatest passion. He was fortunate in inheriting a delectable though neglected site, originally laid out by Repton, with ground that sloped gently down to two large ponds. Here, with the help of his charming and capable wife, he created a garden of real beauty and distinction. Then alpines bit him, and one could count on finding him almost any afternoon in his greenhouse. 'Now here's an amazing little beast, Blunt,' he would say, pointing to some tiny cluster of dreary leaves that cowered behind a hefty zinc label; and I, who had not yet come to know the fascination of mini-horticulture, found his enthusiasm difficult to share or understand.

Talbot was alleged to be musical, and rumour had it that he had even been heard to sing lieder. 'You know, Blunt,' he said to me, more than once, 'that man Brahms shot across an amazing amount of big stuff. Take your Mainacht, for example ...' He always urged me to take my (or rather, his) Mainacht; I think he had little else to offer. He did, however, encourage music, made very welcome the artists who came down to give recitals, and so captivated the violinist Adila Fachiri that, to our great pleasure, she threw her arms round him and embraced him in front of the whole school.

There was a strain of the know-all in Talbot. It was very characteristic of him, for example, that he should write to inform Adila Fachiri that since her last visit some acoustic plaster had been added to the end wall of Big School, and that she would no doubt wish to 'alter her bowing'. Her use of fiddle-bow? Her manner of acknowledging applause? It was hard to see how acoustic plaster could affect either ...

No doubt Talbot did a certain amount of teaching in school, though probably no more than he could help. He had a single lecture, on 'spinning tops', which with little persuasion he would give to almost any Haileybury society that invited him – a perusal of back numbers of 'The Haileyburian' reveals that he delivered it almost annually. I hear it once, and my recollection of it is that the tops behaved very capriciously. He was always so much better with people than with things ...

Talbot's bonhomie pervaded Haileybury. I like best to recall him as he walked among us in the Quad, a smile or a friendly word for even the humblest of us. 'I don't like the look of things in Manchuria, Blunt,' he might say, and pass on before I had time to comment. If only, I thought, we could lend him to Manchuria for a fortnight, then all would be well. But of course it would not have been; for a 'sweet disorder' was inseparable from all he touched, and in next to no time he would have reduced Manchuria to charming chaos.

Wilfrid went to Florence to find a singing teacher 'to infuse a little bel canto and morbidezza' into his 'now rather stolid Teutonic voice' (actually not at all bad). Through the good offices of the ubiquitous Carlo Placci – sometimes known, because of his wide circle of acquaintance, as 'the man who had known the Unknown Soldier' – he was found lodgings and enrolled among the pupils of Signora Minicucci.

It was at the Palazzo Rucellai that I first sampled Florentine entertainment. I had met the Contessa, very soon after my arrival, over a cup of tea at Carlo's. This astounding octogenarian Cossack, red of wig and farded of face, had said to me as she was leaving, 'Do please come to us next Wednesday, Mr Blunt. Carlo will tell you where we live. Just a few friends. Eight o'clock.'

I turned up punctually in my dinner jacket and rang the bell. Double doors sprang instantly apart as if to an 'Open Sesame!', disclosing what might have been a set for the second act of 'Der Rosenkavalier'. I passed between a double row of footmen in eighteenth-century liveries and was deposited in a vast and empty salone where I was left to my own devices. The Contessa appeared about a quarter to nine, and the first guest soon after. At ten o'clock we sat down to supper on the terrace. There were about eighty of us, and I was the only man not in tails. My right-hand neighbour was a Contessa Gravina, whose name meant nothing to me. Hearing that I had come to Florence to study music, she expressed interest: 'You see,' she said, 'my grandfather and my stepfather were musicians.' It did not occur to me to ask their names, which I later discovered to be – as everyone else in Florence of course knew – Liszt and Wagner respectively.

SLOW ON THE FEATHER
FURTHER AUTOBIOGRAPHY
1938–1959

Wilfrid Blunt's second volume of autobiography (1986) covers his years at Eton, where he was Drawing Master for twenty-one years. It's really rather a ragbag – but an attractive one – of Eton life, travel, books, pen portraits of colleagues, and finally a loyal but rueful Postscript about his brother Anthony. Like his great friend Grizel Hartley's book (q.v.), in the main it's for an acquaintance market. There are some memorable characters: in the days when Eton education was incidental to Eton cachet you could carry a few curiosities and a few outright incompetents; now that cachet (in some quarters counter-cachet) becomes incidental to education one imagines they're fairly thin on the ground.

An encounter with Lord Quickswood ('Linky'), Provost from 1936 to 1944:

I was unlucky in that Quickswood was blind and deaf to the beauties of the arts and of nature ... On his attention being drawn one day to a sensational sunset, he considered it for sometime with a puzzled expression and finally observed, 'Yes, extremely tasteful.'

His sermons, though invariably preluded by an apology for his lay status, were delivered with all the authority of the priesthood ... Sometimes Fate tricked him into making them more lively than he intended; yet even when, in a moment of aberration, he announced the 'Narcissus' by mistake for the 'Nunc Dimittis' (a slip that would have interested Freud), none of the congregation was more entertained than he ...

I encountered him one day, near Fellows' Pond, and although he had of course no idea who I was he came up to me and said, 'Do you smell an unpleasant smell?' I sniffed and replied, 'No, sir.' 'Just so. They always say the worst smells don't smell', and he passed on. Presumably the Bursar had reported some suspected effluent from a Slough factory.

Wilfrid's 'The Art of Botanical Illustration' was awarded the Veitch Memorial Gold Medal by the Royal Horticultural Society.

At the same time I organised an exhibition of Flower Books for the National Book League in London. Queen Mary, then in her eighty-fourth year, honoured it with a visit, and my mother greeted her on arrival with a bouquet of gentians, unluckily kicking a fire-bucket in the hall as she curtsied ... Being aware of Her Majesty's amiable tendency to cadge, I presented her with a copy of my book, hoping thereby to forestall any raid on exhibits from my own collection. But she was in acquisitive mood. 'And to whom do those two pretty paintings of heather [by Franz Bauer] belong?' 'To me, Ma'am.' 'They're *very* pretty.' 'Yes, Ma'am.' 'Very pretty indeed ...' I did not yield.

Publishers have endless stories about mistakes in orders for titles. With the first of Wilfrid's books someone asked for 'One Man and His Single Wife' (I suppose the one who meant to mow a widow), and then, after publication of the second volume, there was a trade order for 'Slow on the Father', which – given Wilfrid's declared inclinations – might have been an improvement on the 'Feather'. The public's grasp on literature isn't always tenacious. The Everyman Bookshop in Salisbury, I remember with particular pleasure, had an order for 'Tess of the Dormobiles'.

John Colville

FOOTPRINTS IN TIME

❧

I had published two books by Jock Colville, 'The Portrait of a General' – about a Colville forebear in the Peninsular War, and 'Strange Inheritance' – an entertaining genealogical switchback that started with Ferdinand St Maur, son of the 12th Duke of Somerset, and ended with the last Duke of Portland, with some colourful characters along the way, one of whom was done in by a bear. We thought there might be mileage in reissuing 'Footprints in Time', an exceptionally stylish collection of vignettes that had been published by Collins in 1976, and so it proved. Jock still had up his sleeve, or somewhere more capacious, his 10 Downing Street dairies as Private Secretary to three Prime Ministers, from 1939 to 1955 – a major property, published by Hodder as 'The Fringes of Power'.

Reproduced here are three extracts from 'Footprints in Time'. The first, entitled 'Preux Chevalier', is about Jack Seely.

Faces young and old brightened in the presence of Major-General J. E. B. Seely. He was vain and egotistic, but unfailingly good-natured and open-handed. At the age of six or seven I could count on the immediate gift of half-a-crown every time he saw me. As a result of still more lavish extravagance, the fortune he had inherited from a rich, industrialist father had shrunk to an extent which created some alarm and despondency among the tradesmen who supplied his everyday needs in the Isle of Wight. His gallantry in war was famous and undoubted. He made no effort to disguise the fact because he thought modesty an unnecessary and overrated virtue. He was reputed to have recommended his soldier servant for the VC, 'Standing, as he was, never more than twenty yards behind me throughout the engagement'; and it was said that his readable book of memoirs, 'Fear and Be Slain', had been delayed beyond the expected date of publication because the printer ran out of capital 'I's. He carried on an unceasing war, until personally rebuked by King George V, in order to assert his precedence as Lord Lieutenant of Hampshire over Queen Victoria's daughter, Princess Beatrice, who was Governor of the Isle of Wight. When he was created a peer and assumed the title of Lord Mottistone, the wags at once hailed him as Lord Modest One. Yet none of the stories told against him was repeated with anything but amused affection. His charm and good nature were proof against all malice; and if it be true that the genuinely brave are normally the most reticent about their deeds, Jack Seely was indulgently admitted to be the exception who proved the rule.

Winston Churchill had gone to Harrow when Seely was at the top of the School, a 'blood' as the successful, swashbuckling older boys were described by their admiring juniors. Some fifteen years later Churchill, in his capacity as a newspaper correspondent in the Boer War, was riding his jaded pony across the veldt when he saw a column of British cavalry approaching. Alone, twenty yards ahead of his men, mounted on a black horse and resplendent against the rising sun was Colonel Seely. He seemed to Churchill to represent all that was magnificent in British Imperial power and virtuously bold in the conduct of war. They exchanged greetings and went their respective ways.

Another ten years passed and Churchill, by then First Lord of the Admiralty, entertained the Prime Minister, Mr Asquith, in the Admiralty yacht, 'Enchantress', for a summer cruise in the Mediterranean. Having the Prime Minister trapped for whole fortnight on board a yacht was enormously satisfactory to Churchill. How could the great man possibly avoid discussing all the affairs of State on which Churchill was longing to express his views and exert some influence? But the great man somehow managed it. Day after day went by and every time Churchill tried to bring the conversation round to foreign affairs, or finance, or an Irish Settlement, Asquith would launch into an erudite discussion about the classical antiquities they had been visiting or suggest a game of bridge.

Only on the last evening of the cruise, as 'Enchantress' steamed in a calm sea towards Marseilles, was Churchill given the opening for which he longed. The ladies had gone below to dress for dinner. Asquith and Churchill were sitting on deck in basket chairs. Suddenly Asquith said he felt it essential to make a change at the War Office and was totally unable to decide who the new Secretary of State for War should be. Had Churchill any ideas? The enquiry was unexpected; Churchill had abandoned all hope of serious political conversation, and he was temporarily at a loss. Suddenly there floated before his eyes the 'blood' whom he had so admired at Harrow and the splendid cavalry officer leading his men to war in South Africa. 'What about Jack Seely?' he impetuously volunteered. 'Hm,' said Asquith; 'we should, I think, go and dress for dinner.'

No more was said, but a fortnight later Churchill read in the newspapers that Colonel J. E. B. Seely had been appointed Secretary of State for War.

There followed the Curragh Incident. The British officers stationed in Ireland came close to mutiny in their opposition to the Government's proposal to include Ulster in the plan for Irish Home Rule. Fairly or unfairly, much of the blame fell on the Secretary of State for War, and so after a short, inglorious tenure of office Seely returned to the back benches. Churchill felt that his contribution to Cabinet-making had, to say the least, been of doubtful value; but he never lost his affection for Jack Seely. Indeed, he thought Duff Cooper's wit went too far when, accused across the dining room table of being the worst Secretary of State for War in the present century, he swelled with pretended rage and replied: 'How dare you say that in the presence of Jack Seely?'

One June morning in 1940 I was at my desk at 10 Downing Street, immersed in the frantic activities of those anxious days, when a messenger informed me that Lord Mottistone was at the front door, demanding to see me. 'Bring him in, of course,' I said. The messenger said he had indeed invited him in, but His Lordship had declined. So I went to the front door and there, resplendent in the full dress uniform of a Lord Lieutenant, stood the seventy-year-old General.

'Winston', he said to me, 'is one of my oldest friends. But I don't wish to disturb him at this moment when the future of the world rests on his shoulders.' He fumbled in his pocket and I thought for one moment that he might be going to give me half-a-crown. Instead he brought out a piece of paper on which were written the words: 'Hampshire is behind you.' 'Give that to Winston from me,' he said, and with a gallant smile turned to walk back to Waterloo Station. I gave the Prime Minister the message. He shook with laughter as he read it and then, quite suddenly, he wept.

The second piece is entitled 'A Gift from Cuba'.

The Battle of Britain had been won, but the Battle of the Atlantic hung in the balance. Convoys were being attacked and supply ships were going down by the score. So food, clothing, cigarettes and petrol were rationed and imported luxuries were but memories. Cigars were not held to be necessities, except by the Prime Minister.

His pre-war stock was all but exhausted and since he smoked, or rather consumed, between ten and fifteen a day, as well as being generous in his offers to guests, even the boxes which were frequently sent as presents by friends and admirers were totally inadequate to meet the demand. The situation was approaching the desperate, when one afternoon late in 1940 the Cuban Minister came to Downing Street in a tall-bodied taxi accompanied by a huge cedar-wood cabinet which contained five thousand of the best Havana cigars. It was, he informed a joyful Mr Churchill, a token of the admiration which the Government and people of Cuba felt for the saviour of western civilisation. The sun broke through the clouds.

The next day an official called with the vexatious information that the Prime Minister owed HM Customs and Excise the sum of nearly £10,000 in payment of Customs duty and Purchase Tax. I happened to be on duty and it fell to me to receive this bird of ill-omen. I pointed out that the Prime Ministerial salary was only £10,000 a year. The British public would be disappointed, perhaps even disaffected, if they saw Mr Churchill without a cigar. The official was granite-faced and adamant. The King alone, he said, was exempt from Customs duty: not the Queen or the Queen Mother, and certainly not the Prime Minister.

With trepidation I broke the news. Churchill merely said: 'It is up to you to find a satisfactory solution.'

In such circumstances a man normally turns to God or to his mother. With the greatest reverence for both, I nevertheless felt that neither could be of immediate assistance, and so I fell back upon my Alma Mater, the Foreign Office. I spoke to the Foreign Secretary's Private Secretary. The Prime Minister would, I explained, obviously have to return the cigars and refuse the gift. I supposed this would only lead to a total breakdown of goodwill between the British Empire and Cuba – not perhaps a matter of vital consequence and one must, of course, have one's priorities. But did I not remember seeing in the Foreign Office telegrams a report that the American Government were perturbed about the possible use of Cuban bases by German U-boats? America was not a belligerent and if we did not mind, perhaps we should not worry if they did.

It had the desired effect. That very day an official letter went from the Foreign Office, written on behalf of Mr Secretary Eden, to inform the Lord Commissioners of the Treasury that it was of the greatest importance, on political grounds, not to give offence to the Government of Cuba in this matter. The Lord Commissioners gave way with good grace; the requisite instructions were sent to the Customs: Churchill kept his cigars; and I kept my job. Moreover, a happy precedent was established. Every succeeding year until the war ended, a beautiful cedar-wood box was delivered to No. 10 by the Cuban Minister as continued evidence of the admiration his Government and people felt for Churchill; and every year it was admitted duty free. The Chancellor of the Exchequer and the Foreign Secretary had to pay duty on gifts they received from abroad;

but then the sums in question would not have consumed their entire Ministerial salaries, nor were they national monuments.

The third piece is an abstract from 'The American Connexion', about Averell Harriman, at the time Jock met him Roosevelt's Personal Representative in Britain.

I first saw him [Averell Harriman] in March 1941. Churchill invited him to dine at No. 10, together with Drexel Biddle, American Ambassador to the whole host of our fugitive allies who had established their governments-in-exile in London. After dinner there was a heavy raid and so Churchill, by way of entertaining his guests and his staff, ordered us all to put on tin helmets and led us up to the roof of the Air Ministry to watch the display. For Harriman it was a good introduction to life with Churchill, and he did not turn a hair.

He was often invited to accompany Churchill on his travels and I well remember his presence at Plymouth, just after a devastating raid, at Bristol and at Liverpool. I don't think he was asked for any reason other than the pleasure of his company and the fact that he had unofficially, and almost inadvertently, become an adopted member of Churchill's entourage. As he did not, like Harry Hopkins, lose Roosevelt's personal favour and confidence, his energies were soon required for so many other ploys, such as haggling with Stalin, that later in the war he had less time for constant attendance on the Prime Minister; but, like Winant, he was never far away.

Without knowing it, Harriman saved my life. When he devoted his energies to something, he was only content to excel. In the world of sport he would not rest until he was expert. Thus he had been one of America's best polo players and was a champion at croquet. On the lawn at Chequers he totally defeated Mrs Churchill at croquet, a feat never before witnessed by anybody present. He even played six-pack bézique well. Now it happened that on board the 'Queen Mary', returning from the Second Quebec Conference, I re-taught the Prime Minister bézique, a game he had played many years before but had entirely forgotten. This was a serious error of judgment on my part because for the next twenty years I frequently found myself playing bézique at hours of the morning when I should have preferred to be in bed and asleep.

In January 1945, Churchill proposed to take two of his Private Secretaries, John Martin and Leslie Rowan, to the Yalta Conference. A few nights before the party was due to leave, Churchill had finished all the work he intended to do, had read the next day's morning papers and was, I hoped, about to say good night, when he suddenly felt an urge to play bézique. At about 3 a.m. he announced that as the Yalta Conference was bound to have its longueurs, I had better come too. A few games of bézique would be an agreeable contrast to Plenary Meetings and neither Martin nor Rowan, remarkable though all their other qualities were, knew how to play the game. It was not mine to reason why; but next morning my colleagues were far from gratified by the news. It meant that the office in London would be understaffed and anyhow there was no room in the Prime Minister's plane. I should have to travel separately in a York transport aircraft which would be conveying some other members of the so-called 'Argonaut' party to the Crimea.

The night before our departure, Averell Harriman came to dine with Churchill. He could, it seemed, play bézique. He was, no doubt, as great a master of the game as he was of polo and croquet. There was therefore no need for me to go to Yalta after all and, said Churchill, it had been forcefully represented to him that my absence would leave the office short-handed in London. I unpacked; I was disappointed; I was privately indignant with Martin and Rowan, devoted though I was to both of them, and felt that they had behaved in a curmudgeonly way. As for Harriman, it seemed the worst luck in the world that in addition to his other skills he should know how to play bézique. I was wrong on all counts, for the York, on which I should have flown, crashed off Pantellaria and its passengers were killed.

Jessica Douglas-Home

ONCE UPON ANOTHER TIME

❧

It was Jessica Douglas-Home's husband, Charles, whose report and brief arrest first alerted the West to the Soviet invasion of Czechoslovakia. Later, after being appointed editor of 'The Times', he became terminally ill and Jessica's commitment to helping the dissident communities in Czechoslovakia, Poland, Hungary and Romania coincided in the early stages with the increasingly distressing circumstances of that illness. Certainly there was a body of supposedly intelligent opinion in the West which regarded any intervention behind the Iron Curtain as more likely to be an embarrassment than an inspiration to those it was intended to support. After reading 'Once Upon Another Time' you will tend to find that argument unpersuasive. Smuggling in volumes of Plotinus, too, may seem a little low key in comparison with arming the dissidents with rather more overtly destructive weapons (though if your game is Greek translation and you catch Plotinus in obliquer mood you may find that comparison less well-defined). But the hazards were all too real. The story is well, and modestly, told. This is someone with the courage of her convictions; and if like me – indeed probably like a lot of us – you have not much courage and fairly muddled convictions, you can only admire her spirit and her sense of principle.

My plane landed many hours late on the night of 23 September 1987 in Bucharest's Otopeni airport – a ramshackle, ill-lit, concrete structure. Since nobody but my mother and the Romanian visa section in Kensington knew my flight details, I was disconcerted by the sound of my name being called repeatedly around the dilapidated terminal; and even more so when I was located by a pretty and immaculately dressed young woman who presented me with red carnations 'to welcome my arrival' and instantly disappeared. Had the Romanian communities in Paris or London been infiltrated? Was this a Judas kiss to identify me to a distant watcher? Or was it merely a mark of recognition of my late husband's name? I never knew. It was typical of the mystery that was to envelop my every experience in Romania.

The chief purpose of my visit was to find the 78-year-old Professor Constantin Noica, who had recently been propelled into the political limelight through two books by his pupil Gabriel Liiceanu recording philosophical dialogues at Noica's country retreat. Tales of Noica's ascetic way of life had reached me from Romanian expatriates. Liiceanu portrayed him as a Socratic figure, self-critical and generous, seeking enlightenment through reading, meditation and dialectical discussion. His calm rejection of ambiguity, after years of lies and half-truths, gave Romanians a glimpse of another world. Liiceanu's books generated a ferment in Bucharest and enraged the authorities.

In Czechoslovakia, Poland and Hungary there had been a network of friendships to fall back on: in Romania I had to rely on second-hand introductions. This left me uneasy. However many times I had been assured by exiles that such-and-such a person would want to see me, I knew how changeable individual circumstances could be under Ceauşescu's reign of terror. There was the additional concern that the Third Directorate of the political police had enforced a decree that made it a criminal offence to talk to foreigners without filing a report.

Before I went in search of Noica I had a call to make in Bucharest. After a sleepless night I dressed inconspicuously and set out on foot up Calea Victoriei to the north-east sector of the city. If I were followed, I would have no difficulty in detecting my pursuer. There were so few people. Empty side streets, no stalls, no cafés, no bustle, no life. Where was everybody? Only two vans went by during my walk. Private cars had been banned in Bucharest since January.

I turned right into the wide main road of Boulevard Dacia, slipped through a courtyard into a block of flats, climbed a staircase to the first floor and steeled myself to knock on the door of Flat 15, marked Celac-Botez. I heard footsteps coming towards me; the door opened a crack; dark eyes met mine in a blank stare. I whispered the name of Michnea Berindei as introduction and was ushered in. Mariana Celac's soft-spoken welcome soothed my anxiety. In a subsequent pencil drawing I recorded my first impression of her sitting at her desk, her thick, straight haircut, with its heavy fringe, framing a wide face that exuded authority and intelligence. 'Her flat', I wrote afterwards in my diary, 'is a combination of all the ones I know belonging to dissidents, whether in Prague, Cracow, Brno or Budapest ... the same austere atmosphere ... a feeling of peace as if I had come home; the bookcases, the shelves, the desk, the darkness and lack of clutter, nothing on the walls except objects of intense significance.'

A few weeks earlier Mariana's husband, Mihai Botez, had left to make a new life in the United States. This was a disappointment, for as recently as May I had read an interview in the 'Christian Science Monitor' in which he criticised those who fled the country: 'When dissidents protest, face persecution, and then leave for the West, the Government can say that we only want to get the better living conditions on the other side. If 1,000 of us intellectuals would stay then we would have an impact.' Three months after the article, however, he and his wife had come to a decision: as a mathematician of international repute, Mihai would emigrate to America, while Mariana, who felt that she would not be able to re-establish herself abroad as a practising architect, would stay behind to look after her mother. They had no children.

The last ten years had been a severe test of their endurance. They belonged to a generation which had been optimistic for the Ceauşescu regime in its early years, seeing in it a promise of modernisation and openness to Western ideas. The youngest Romanian ever to receive a doctorate in mathematics, Mihai had become the party's top economics adviser but had developed serious doubts over Ceauşescu's policies. In 1977 he lost all his positions, including that of professor at Bucharest University. Reduced to the rank of researcher, he refused to be silenced, hoping that through his example the status of the dissident intellectual might be regularised 'so that he may live, work and travel in dignity, tolerated, if not wholly accepted, by the authorities'.

In 1979 Radio Free Europe had broadcast a penetrating critique of Ceauşescu's economic strategy. Mihai Botez was the acknowledged author. Taking pains to appear as non-confrontational as possible, he avoided a general attack on the regime, concentrating on specific blunders, including the Danube canal. The evening after the broadcast Mihai, Mariana and eighteen others who had clubbed together to buy tickets were due to attend the first of a series of concerts in Bucharest. Arriving at Athéné Hall, the Botezes made their way to their seats to find that not one of their friends had turned up. They sat alone in two empty rows. That night they went on foot to each of their friends' apartments, dropping notes through the letter boxes. Nobody was to worry, they wrote: neither of them would be going to any more concerts in the series. The Botezes were never again received in their once wide circle. Mariana was demoted to a lowly position in her architectural practice, while Mihai was banished from the university altogether. By June 1987 his situation had deteriorated further. He was twice physically attacked in the street at night by unidentified men in plain clothes. It was then he first contemplated emigration.

Mariana's plain kitchen looked to have been untouched since the 1930s. Over a cup of herb tea, I went straight to the point, explaining to her the concept of an underground university. She surprised me by responding calmly and immediately that she believed herself to be the person to act as the focal point for our network. She emphasised what we would be letting ourselves in for and warned – as much, it seemed, for herself as for me – of the slowness of the journey and the pain it would entail. Visitors should only make contact with one Romanian at a time. It would be folly, and anyway impossible, to attempt seminars as in Czechoslovakia. She could provide an example from that very morning – an artist friend of hers who had been telephoned by an Australian who was briefly visiting Bucharest, but had been too scared even to return the call.

It seemed almost too good to be true that at my first effort I had stumbled across the key figure I was looking for. Privately I wondered how Mariana would be able to meet foreigners without incurring reprisals. Perhaps, like Pavel Bratinka, she was effectively protected by family connections – her brother Sergiu had for years been Ceauşescu's interpreter and was later to be Romania's ambassador in London. (After the dictator's execution, Sergiu Celac had his own image removed from all photographs where they appeared together.) We agreed to meet again on my return from my pilgrimage to Professor Noica, who lived in the northern mountain village of Păltiniş.

I awoke at 3.30 am from a fitful night and started at once for the town of Sibiu in my hired car, a grey Dacia, the Romanian version of a small Renault. It had proved impossible to buy a map, but Mariana had given me instructions. The first hour of the journey I wasted looking for the main road out of Bucharest. The street lighting was permanently switched off, except on the routes travelled by Ceauşescu, but even if I could have seen anything there were no road signs.

Long before dawn the car headlights picked out queues forming in front of empty bread shops, perhaps awaiting deliveries. On the rare occasion when a street name appeared, I had to get out of the car to read it. Even at this early hour there were masses of people going to work, but when I asked in my incomprehensible Romanian the way to Piteşti, the response was always apprehensive and unhelpful. At last one woman, plucking up the courage to speak to a foreigner, pointed me in the right direction. As the road deteriorated into deep ruts past Pitesti, I was thwarted by a series of slowly-moving carts, some drawn by oxen, some by horses. I braked repeatedly, on the brink of collision, alerted almost too late by the tiny lantern-jar on a stick that each cart carried at the back. At 8.30 I arrived in Sibiu. From there I took the track to Păltiniş, driving through the village of Răşinari, where each house on the cobbled main street was painted a beautiful pale yellow or green.

Noica was a marked man and I made no attempt to disguise my visit. His house, however, was hard to find. A friendly villager offered to lead me on foot through a wood up a steep mountain path strewn with pine needles. After twenty minutes' walking we reached a plateau, where my guide quietly disappeared. Ahead of me stood a hut made out of trees hewn in long flat slices. I knocked on a red painted door at the front. Noica appeared above me on a balcony, dressed in a faded green quilted jacket and brown leather spats. With nothing more than a mildly surprised look, he came down the rough flight of stairs, showing no sign of his age, and invited me up into a small room which served as his library, bedroom, washroom and workroom. In one corner stood a tall ceramic stove.

I knew the bare bones of his life story already. Having taught in Bucharest before the Communist takeover, he was exiled to a provincial town and later, ostensibly on account of a book on Goethe, charged with 'plotting against the social order' and sentenced to imprisonment and the seizure of his assets. After three years in gaol he was adopted by Amnesty as a Prisoner of Conscience, but it was a further three years before he was released. He accepted persecution as his lot and never sought the international recognition which emigration might have brought him, as it had brought his friends and contemporaries Mircea Eliade and Eugene Ionescu.

Noica's room had neither desk nor bookshelves – he did his writing on a wooden tray. On the floor and on the bed piles of letters, journals and reference books were arranged in orderly lines. At first he teased me that I had been sent as a spy, but then he was serious. Out of a striped shopping bag made of meshed plastic he methodically unloaded his life's work, about fourteen books. He commented on each one in turn. The book for which he had been arrested, 'A Study of Goethe', was incomplete, the missing part of the text having been destroyed by the Securitate. It was a measure of his isolation that he wished to tell me every detail.

We spoke in French, occasionally breaking into German when either of us was stuck. It was not hard to understand why the younger generation so venerated him. On his rare excursions to Bucharest he always drew a crowd of disciples, on whom he impressed the life or death importance of retaining, at no matter what cost, the links which bound their country to European civilisation. Had he spent his life in exile, he used to tell them, he could never have written 'The Romanian Sense of Self'. This was his most profound work, in which he set out to rescue Romania from the lethal influence of Newspeak.

After a while we went to a house further up the hill, whose occupant served Noica a daily meal. As we swallowed a watery vegetable soup, I told him why I had come so far to see him. I needed his personal stamp of approval for my proposals. He listened attentively to what I had to say, nodding appreciatively and looking me directly in the eye. When I returned to Bucharest, he told me, I must make contact with his trusted pupils, Andrei Pleşu and Gabriel Liiceanu. These two, above all, would help mould my plans. When the time was right one of his followers would emerge to unite the fragmented and fearful society in which they were trapped. Meanwhile, his own task was to give meaning to the life of the philosopher, offering an example of man's ability to attain inner peace when the external conditions seemed beyond redemption.

SINS OF COMMISSION

WILLIAM DOUGLAS HOME

I commissioned Peter Brookes to draw a tank with a knot in its gun. Some military pundit then pointed out that it was the wrong sort of tank, so I was obliged to include a facetious disclaimer under his credit: 'Cover drawing by Peter Brookes. Any letters from General Headstrong, Major McTrack or Colonel Gorge-Cheddar-Gorge pointing out that it should have been modelled on a Churchill rather than a Crusader tank will not be forwarded.'

William Douglas Home

SINS OF COMMISSION

❧

During the Normandy campaign that followed the D-day landings in 1944 William Douglas Home, as an officer in a tank regiment, refused to obey an order that he thought would involve the civilian population of Le Havre in unnecessary casualties. It resulted in court martial and a spell of imprisonment in Wormwood Scrubs and Wakefield Prison. It turned out, after William's mother died, that his parents had kept all his wartime letters home and he proposed them as this book. We liked the title; William was well known as a playwright; and the content, often flippant, recorded a serious predicament of conscience. It came out in 1985 and proved to make commercial sense. And our dealings were infectiously enjoyable.

He writes to his parents from Wormwood Scrubs.

Dear Pa and Ma,

No doubt forgetting that the crest of the Honourable Society of Censors is Mr Baldwin's lips (rouge and sealed) dexter to a dragon couchant (Mrs Baldwin), the Deputy Governor informed me that my last letter to you was that of a peevish child. Reading between the lines of the Bible, I judge that there may have been a note of petulance in the first letter that Samson, after chewing up the pillars of the temple, penned to his mamma. As for childishness, it is a pity that I have to change that style, which has ranged from 'I am quite well. I made 2 yesterday' of 23 years ago to the winged words of recent years – with such success and mutual satisfaction. I tell you this lest you should wonder why the atmosphere of this epistle is like that of Mr Gladstone writing to his creditors.

William was transferred from Wormwood Scrubs to Wakefield Prison. In May 1945

my parents came to see me – in the ping-pong table room, as I had forecast. When they left (my mother wrote and told me later), she had got into the taxi at the gate, only to see my father walking down outside the prison wall towards a big house. 'Where're you going, Charlie?' she called. 'Hold on, Lil,' he called back, 'I'm just going along to thank the dear little Governor for having William here.'

As soon as they had gone William wrote to his parents:

It was delightful seeing you yesterday. You will now realise what I mean when I talk of the awkwardness of prison visits. However much one tries, it is impossible to talk about anything but trivial things. First of all the time is too short and one spends all one's time trying to remember the things one wanted to say, and, secondly, the shock of seeing people one knows after months of confinement is too great to be overcome in half an hour. That is why when a soldier or anyone else returns home after a long absence the first thing he does is to sink into a chair and let the full enjoyment come over him gradually, and he speaks when the spirit moves him. Nor, when meeting his parents for the first time for a year and a half, does he go out into the street and ask the first policeman he sees to come and share the moment, however charming the policeman may be in private life.

The prison commissioners still think otherwise, and endeavour to force into half an hour a social and emotional interlude which cannot be so treated. And if ever I get onto the prison reform committees, I shall emphasise the mental processes of prisoners, and shall display from my own experience the shock any home or family influence has on a prisoner by telling the unbelieving that when I got your first letter and saw it lying on the table in my cell, believe it or not, the tears streamed down my face onto a portion of the floor in Wormwood Scrubs. Had the officer looked through the peephole in that door at that moment, he would doubtless have thought I was washing down my cell.

William's parents were treated to a final benign gloss on custodial sentence.

H. M. Prison
Wakefield
12.6.45

Dear Lord Home,

I am much obliged to you for your kind letter of the 9th instant. Your son left here in good spirits and I think his experience has not injured him in any way.

There are limits to the things which may (or may not) be done in places of this kind, but I believe your son left us without any bitterness in his heart.

I have shown your letter to Mrs Smith.

With kind regards to Lady Home and to you.

I remain,

Yours sincerely,

W. SMITH

The Rt. Hon. The Earl of Home, K.T., T.D.,
The Hirsel
Coldstream

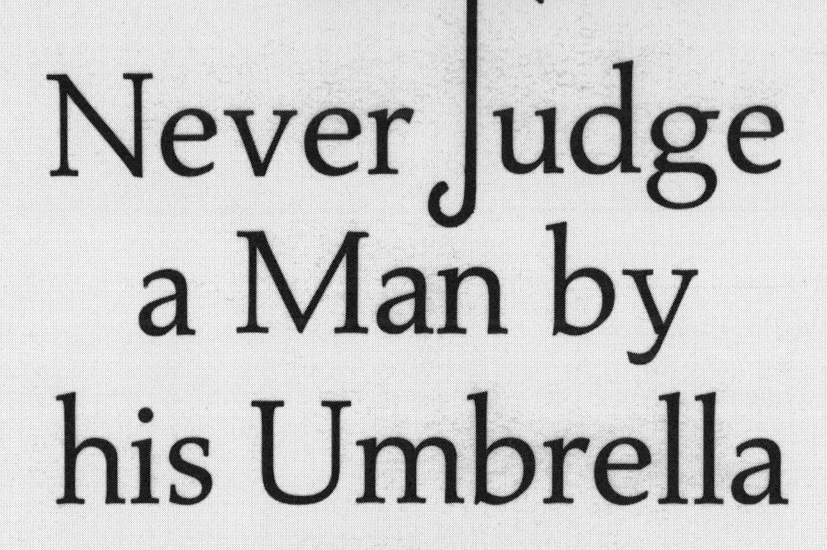

Cream background, black lettering, red fabric on umbrellas

Nicholas Elliott

NEVER JUDGE A MAN BY HIS UMBRELLA

❧

The provenance for the title was a notice in an Eton master's schoolroom: 'Never judge a man by his umbrella. It may not be his.' I pressed for it because it was a typographic natural, with the 'j' of 'judge' just asking to be the handle of the opened umbrella and a horizontal folded umbrella the natural division between title and author on the front cover (see illustration). Besides, it amused and puzzled people. It was a good choice.

Another promotional advantage was that we were forbidden by MI6 to divulge anywhere that Nicholas had been a senior officer in that organisation; so the first thing any journalist or reviewer was going to say was how ridiculous that was. Assisting his old office in withholding from the public something they already knew was, as I described it in the blurb to Nicholas's follow up volume, 'rather like a man holding his cards dutifully close to his chest but the wrong way round'. Still, it would be an immediate peg for drawing attention to the book without serious risk of bringing national security to its knees.

Nicholas was an excellent raconteur (which doesn't by any means make a good author). I know humour is very much in the eye – or rather ear – of the beholder, but he had a bottomless fund of anecdote and a developed sense of the absurd. He was also obsessed with divining rods. He drew our attention to huge (and still undiscovered) treasure under the corner of one of our barns, but his only major success was to locate his lady doctor's missing passport which had slipped down behind her writing desk.

His father, Claude, had been Head Master of Eton and the relationship between father and son is affectionately and amusingly caught. The latter part of the book covers his MI6 'travels', including his confrontation of Philby in Beirut (which resulted, I'm afraid, in a dropped catch). After leaving the Service he worked for a time with Tiny Rowland. I insisted that the chapter on Tiny Rowland must be approved in advance. Rowland's lawyers confirmed that the material had been seen by their client. 'Approved' was the word I was looking for, so I told Nicholas that I was both poor and of nervous disposition and a writ from someone famously litigious was not my idea of what the bookmakers used to call 'winnings on the breakfast table'. So we played safe, although I couldn't see much that could have caused offence.

Great-Uncle Edgar was responsible for an encounter between Claude [Nicholas's father] and the poet Swinburne. At the turn of the century Swinburne used to walk every weekday from The Pines in Putney to the Dog and Whistle (as it was then called) in Wimbledon Village. This brought him past the gates of Fernwood, the house of Claude's parents. One spring day Claude, at a tender age, was on a walk with Edgar when they saw Swinburne approaching, a conspicuous figure with his shoulders thrown back and his arms by his side with the palms turned forward. Edgar offered Claude half-a-crown if he would ask Swinburne if he thought the hounds of spring were on winter's traces. Of course Claude at that age would do almost anything for such a sum and after a swift rehearsal with Great-Uncle Edgar (being not yet acquainted with 'Atalanta') he went up to Swinburne and pressed him for a slant on the matter. The poet's only reply was 'Go away, you nasty little boy', but Claude got his half-crown.

When Nicholas was young his father was a don at Jesus College, Cambridge.

G [Nicholas's mother] never really took to Cambridge life though she made many friends there and entertained well. She became very fond of racing and used often to go to Newmarket. At one stage

Claude bought her a small car; she tried hard to learn to drive but finally gave up having allegedly been passed in one afternoon by a hearse, a pig, and an old lady riding a tricycle. Claude himself was a keen motorist, so much so that he bought a Jaguar on his seventy-second birthday ... He was extremely proud of his first car – a de Dion Bouton which he had bought second hand in about 1907. It had previously belonged to a famous actress, possibly Lily Elsie. There was one single headlight in front. Inside were two levers. One was the brake, the other released a mechanism which caused an instrument to play the first few lines of 'O God Our Help in Ages Past'.

At Eton

Many of us, myself included, got into financial difficulties, but there was one boy who devised a most ingenious way of extricating himself. He put a notice in the 'Windsor, Slough & Eton Gazette' along with the following lines: 'How to make milk puddings without having to use milk. Send SAE and 1/- worth of stamps.' The local housewives could not wait to find out and replies came in by the score. The boy cashed all the stamps at the Eton post office and put a reply in all the SAEs saying 'Use cream instead'. This was unfavourably received by the housewives and the Slough police were called in to investigate.

As a boy I was always rather in awe of Leo Amery when he came to stay with my parents, though I came to like him very much indeed. Julian has a delightful story of his father. In the later stages of the First World War Lloyd George had asked him to go to Paris to ask Clemenceau if he would agree to the French Ambassador in London, M. Cambon, undertaking a highly delicate mission to the United States. Leo Amery had approached 'the Tiger' with some trepidation, to be told that he fully agreed that M. Cambon was entirely suitable but that he could not bring himself to ask him. M. Cambon, he added, was in a state of acute personal distress because 'the greatest tragedy' had befallen him 'that could befall any Frenchman'. To Leo Amery's tactful inquiry as to what this was, Clemenceau had replied: 'His mistress's husband has died.'

In Egypt

There was no time for sightseeing. On one occasion, however, I did take an American girl to dinner at Mena House and afterwards, under a full moon, we strolled out arm in arm to look at the pyramids. 'Don't you think they look terribly romantic?' I asked. She replied that she thought they looked like a couple of slag heaps.

Relations with Egyptians in wartime were never easy, because of the arrogant British attitude in those days of regarding them a 'bloody wogs'. Many years later someone remarked that one should not be too hard on their army as it had not won a battle since the second act of 'Aïda'.

WITH MY LITTLE EYE
OBSERVATIONS ALONG THE WAY

The title of this follow-up volume to 'Never Judge a Man by his Umbrella' escaped stricture from MI6. Perhaps they didn't appreciate the allusion. It was a fairly lightweight but an entertaining – and occasionally risqué – assortment with one or two serious pieces (on the affair of Commander Crabb, for instance) interspersed.

I liked a remark in one of my friend Robert Moss's novels: 'It was such a one-horse town that even the local whore was still a virgin.'

'I like a Martini,' said Mabel,
'But I've learned to take two at the most.
For with three I'm under the table
And with four I'm under my host.'

On wartime Turkey:

Apart from a daily and uncertain flight by Turkish Airlines to Cyprus and Cairo – uncertain because the airline did not normally fly if there were any clouds in the sky – the Taurus 'Express' provided the only reliable means of getting from Turkey into the Middle East. Consequently, the wagons-lits conductors were much in demand by the Axis powers as spies.

They were a colourful lot and normally took the precaution of clearing their yardarms with the Secret Police who were perfectly content to let them spy on condition that they reported in detail on the briefs they were given and by whom. One enterprising fellow managed to get himself profitably recruited by the Abwehr, the Sicherheitsdienst, the Italian military, naval and air attachés and the Japanese military attaché, all unknown to one another. One of these conductors, whom I will call Herbert, worked for the British and reported one day that he had been recruited by the Abwehr to pick up a wireless set on the platform at Adana and deliver it to a man who would identify himself with a match between his front teeth on the train's arrival at Mosul platform. Herbert was given to understand that this was an operation of the utmost importance involving the sabotage of the Mosul oilfields and that he would be well rewarded.

Telegrams flew all over the place. There was a complication in that Herbert, although he had insured himself with his own people, flatly refused to take the wireless set through the Turkish-Iraqi customs himself – very wisely in my view. Complicated arrangements thus had to be made whereby a British diplomatic courier had to go on the train, be handed a wireless set after Herbert had been given it on Adana platform and then insert it at the bottom of a sealed diplomatic bag and sew it up. An appropriate courier was found and documented and after a sewing lesson departed on the train in the next carriage to Herbert. To start with all went according to plan. Herbert took possession of the set at Adana, handed it to our courier who inserted it into the bottom of the diplomatic bag and sewed it in. A disaster then occurred that could not reasonably have been envisaged by the most meticulous of planners. Herbert's coach, the last one on the train, came off the rails and was left behind. The courier of course had no choice but to go on, later to perceive a highly agitated and swarthy individual pacing up and down Mosul platform with a match between his teeth. In due course the individual departed, under observation of course by the British Security authorities, but escaped their vigilance and vanished into the *suq*, never to be seen again.

The operation was thus a complete fiasco both for the Germans and the British; and all Herbert could do was to return the set to his Abwehr contact. Meanwhile, a Turkish intelligence officer, of a philosophical turn of mind, remarked that all was not lost – after all Allah was not an Armenian.

And finally a little verse which we headed, of course, NEVER JUDGE A MAN ...

The rain it raineth every day
Upon the just and unjust fellah;
But mostly on the just because
The unjust has the just's umbrella.

W. A. Elliott

ESPRIT DE CORPS: A SCOTS GUARDS OFFICER ON ACTIVE SERVICE 1943–1945

❧

John Keegan picked this up in the 'Daily Telegraph', where he made it his Choice of the Year: 'This is a brilliant book, perfectly written, spare, understated ... Young people overlook how awful the Second World War was for a fighting regiment. Old men remember.' Lieutenant General Sir James Wilson, writing in the 'Army Quarterly and Defence Journal', endorsed the view: 'A marvellous account of what infantry fighting in a really good battalion against top class opposition is really like ... A monument to the human spirit.' Archie Elliott's war diary was not kept with a view to publication, but its interest lies not only in its graphic account of the 2nd Battalion's involvement from the Salerno landings in Italy to the end of the war in Europe, but also its insights into how intense loyalties came to be formed and how a particular battalion maintained its morale throughout constant fighting. Archie Elliott himself, now a retired Scottish judge, was captured just after the Salerno landings but escaped with a fellow officer, Ian Fraser, the following day. Oddly, Ian Fraser's book, 'The High Road to England', also came my way and describes the same incident.

It was shortly after the landings that things went badly wrong.

My company had only reached its objective because we had been able to use the tunnel under the embankment to move right in under our barrage before the Germans had time to recover. Also because there was such a mix-up in the darkness that the Germans did not know who was who and where to shoot. Meanwhile, oblivious of the fact that we were the only company to capture its objective, we strutted about as proud as peacocks in the midst of a still intact German battalion heavily supported by tanks.

8 Platoon now crossed the road on to the fields beyond and started to try to dig in; but the ground was as hard as concrete and they only had entrenching tools. As the moon rose I sent Chadwick's section in the direction of the crossroads, which was now a hundred yards to our left, wishing to know if the shouting and noise of tracked vehicles coming from that direction meant the arrival of 'G' Company. Suddenly Chadwick shouted to look out as there were tanks coming straight down the road at us. I didn't react at once, thinking these might be our own Shermans. There was a sinister grinding and squeaking of bogie wheels and two German tanks or half-tracks came clattering straight for us down the tarmac. The road was a death trap with high barbed wire fences on either side and our Piat (anti-tank projector) was with platoon headquarters. Cursing the moonlight, I yelled at everyone to lie face downwards at the side of the road, trusting the tank driver's lack of vision. I could feel all my muscles contracting with fear as the metal tracks passed within yards of my elbow scattering sparks in all directions. The tanks, however, passed straight on over the bridge beside 7 Platoon. ...

Things were now beginning to get out of hand. I told my leading section to get quickly into a house (which, unknown to me, was full of Germans) and ran back to try to find my platoon HQ ... I only got as far as my second section when I saw some more tanks approaching from the other direction with the moonlight glinting on their turrets. To my horror I realised that they were not simply motoring through us again but were part of a coordinated infantry-supported counter-attack. Long lines of German infantry stretched behind them, coming in from our right side and rear ... The tables were now completely turned and the rest was a humiliating fiasco.

After lying in a ditch for two hours within twenty yards of a German post, Archie and his companions were captured. 'I must confess that my first feelings on capture were not of shame but of immense relief at being still alive.'

To pass the time I chatted in doggerel German to a genial guard with a pleasant face who turned out to be an ex-ski-instructor from Austria, where, so he said, he used to meet many English whom he liked. I asked him what German soldiers thought of our soldiers and he replied, 'Brave, but stupid.' His division had not fought us before and he told me they had just come south from fighting the Russians at Rostov. I asked him what the fighting had been like on the Eastern Front and he said it all depended on whether you could get good billets in the winter. In Poland the inhabitants' houses had been just passable but those of the Russian peasants were beyond description and mostly unfit for habitation. He conceded however, that they were fanatical soldiers. He asked if I would like to see some Russian soldiers captured at Stalingrad. His 16th Panzer Division apparently used these ex-Soviet soldiers as mess orderlies. One of them was brought forward to speak to me. He had a roguish smiling face with Slav features but could speak little German. He said he came from Kubishev. I asked him why he was now wearing German uniform after taking part in the heroic defence of Stalingrad. He merely laughed and replied, 'Good food, good pay!' He was obviously a bit of a comic and the Germans ragged him playfully as if he were a tame dog.

Shortly after this Archie and Ian Fraser, on their way with a column of prisoners to German Divisional Headquarters, managed to slip away from their captors and eventually made their way back to the British lines.

There is an illuminating passage on the theme of esprit de corps when 201 Guards Brigade, short of reinforcements, was sent home to be regrouped for the expected Second Front. Training in Scotland, they were joined by some 1,500 of the disbanded RAF Regiment – most 'anti-Army and anti-Brigade of Guards in particular, so they marched up the hill to our camp chanting, "We are the RAF, RAF, RAF!"' How the great majority were infused with regimental allegiance is bruising but instructive.

And so the fighting began again, pushing into Germany itself in the last months of the war. Archie and Alastair Erskine were the only two rifle platoon officers still surviving who had landed with the Battalion at Salerno; and Erskine was to be killed too, the day before he was due to be transferred to Divisional Headquarters as a liaison officer.

The chief weakness of the German defence strategy in this northern part of Germany was that it was designed on the supposition that their Volksturm or Home Guard would sabotage our supply lines and that the local people would give the Wehrmacht every assistance. In fact the Volksturm, in so far as it existed at all, never fired a shot. The farm people too were quite ready to point out German minefields for us to clear so that they could get on with the proper job of tending their animals and mending their homesteads. Most agricultural labour on the farms through which we were now passing appeared to be done by foreign prisoners on parole living in the German farmhouses. Mostly these were Russians, still wearing Russian uniforms, who persisted in saluting me as an officer when they popped up from behind hedges. But surprisingly some were also French prisoners wearing French uniforms. There were no British or Americans.

When were about to move off, the squadron commander of our company/squadron battle group came up and asked me to get my men immediately on top of his tanks preparatory to motoring straight up last night's road past the very wood from which we had been fired on. I do not think he had personally seen what happened ... I expostulated and said this needed a set-piece attack as there was no reason whatsoever to suppose the Germans had withdrawn. Only those in front could know whether they had or had not done so. He became angry and said we were to advance together up the road and that if I did not mount his tanks at once they would continue without us. I therefore said I would be prepared to put my infantry on the second but not on the leading tank, to which he eventually agreed.

As my men had heard this heated argument I felt in honour bound to put myself on the second (i.e. the first infantry-laden) tank where, however, I sat on the left-hand protected side of its turret.

So we set off straight up the road towards the very wood where the Germans had been firmly entrenched but which was really the objective of 'F' Company following behind. The distance narrowed to a hundred yards and still no sign of the enemy. Then the leading tank started to pass alongside the wood itself with the commander's head protruding from its turret. Still no German reaction. I now began to feel a complete fool who would have to make a public apology to the Welsh Guards squadron commander.

Suddenly a Panzerfaust sailed through the air from the edge of the wood and hit the turret of the leading tank – but without exploding. The Germans had cunningly let it through to render our infantry better targets. Within seconds a hail of bullets raked the top of my tank as I hugged the left side of its turret shouting at the tank commander to stop and let us get off. This seemed to take an age. I could not hear the Spandaus firing for the noise of the tank; but could see men reeling around me from the impact of machine-gun bullets. As I was pressed shoulder to shoulder against Sergeant Ross I could even feel bullets hitting him straight in the chest. Our tanks all veered off the tarmac road into the field on the left and so out of Panzerfaust range. Most of my leading section were shot off the tank, landing right under the Germans' noses, including Sergeant Ross who was mortally wounded. I managed to hang on sideways behind the tank turret and then dropped to the ground as it lurched to a standstill. One could then momentarily stand protected by the tank and watch machine-gun bullets tearing up a furrow on the turf beside it.

The book closes on an elegiac note. The casualty statistics are sickening.

Since the Battalion had crossed the Rhine a month before, the rifle companies had sustained the worst of the casualties, with 17 platoon officers killed and wounded and 223 other ranks. Right Flank alone had lost 95. During the war as a whole the Battalion had now lost 113 officers killed or wounded and 1,246 other ranks – more than in the First World War.

On Sunday 6 May 1945 I attended the Scots/Welsh Group's Service of Remembrance in the old Lutheran church at Stade. The official German surrender had been marked the previous day with a feu de joie from the Corps artillery, firing off all their unused live ammunition. So the war in the West was really over.

The church was of mellow red brick and had stood throughout the centuries. First we heard the National Anthem played by an amateur organist, followed by prayers officially recommended by the Archbishop of Canterbury. Their refrain was; 'Thine is the Victory, O Lord, not mine.' The congregation replied at the end of each prayer: 'We thank thee O Lord.'

Our respected padre, the Revd David Whiteford, then stepped down and the two Commanding Officers of the Scots/Welsh Group presided over the remainder of the service, which was more a memorial to our dead. Standing by the altar each Commanding Officer read out the long list of his battalion's dead in a voice deep with emotion. The Last Post was then sounded by trumpet from outside the great west door, to be followed by two minutes' silence. Then Pipe Major Bain started playing a Scottish lament on his pipes from beside the altar – the 'Flowers of the Forest, that fought aye the foremost, the prime of our land, lie cauld in the clay.'

His piping brought tears to many eyes as he marched slowly through the west door and down the hill, his notes growing fainter and fainter. One thought of graves on the Italian mountains and now along the German roads. But as the piping became more distant it seemed as if the spring breezes played tricks with the lament so that it echoed back sounding more like a Scottish reel. One thought of laughter as the sun went down and of songs around the brew can fires; of Corporal Bryson trying to catch old Gallene [a hen] in the Italian rain, of Sergeant-Major Lumsden roaring drunk at Hogmanay; of laughter in the back of the TCLs and of Support Company trying to pretend there was not a war on.

The 2nd Battalion Scots Guards – they were a terrible mob; but I would not have fought in any other.

Massimo Freccia

THE SOUNDS OF MEMORY

❧

I thought this an attractive book which didn't get the attention it deserved, although one reviewer thought it 'as remarkable a slim [not that slim] volume of memoirs as any to have emerged from the pen of a practising musician'. Massimo Freccia had a successful conducting career and a wide acquaintance in the international musical world.

My family lived in Florence. From my infancy I was brought up in a gloomy fifteenth-century palazzo in the medieval part of town, surrounded by small houses whose ground floors were occupied by blacksmiths and coachmen, who carried out their activities in the narrow streets. These neighbours considerably enlarged my vocabulary, with the result that I was thrown out of the elementary school and entrusted to the care of an English governess. She left six months later in despair, to be followed a long line of tutors. Then one day my brother, Vieri, and I committed an entire legion of lead Roman soldiers to the top of a stove just to watch their annihilation. The gesture was interpreted by my father as defeatist, anarchical, and subversive. A tough Dominican was placed in command of my education.

Vieri was a painter, whimsical, irresponsible and a professional charmer. The young Herbert von Karajan thought he was the most intelligent man he had ever met.

The charm of Paris in the late Twenties was created by a large number of people who expanded in their daily lives more than in their works. Artur Rubinstein, for instance, although in those days a brilliant virtuoso, was more of a celebrity for his immense vitality, his wit as a storyteller, his attraction for women, and his magnetic charm, than for his 'pianisme'. His technique was occasionally at fault for lack of study. It happened once that, having to practise for a future concert, he instructed his butler, Jean, not to bother him with lady admirers' telephone calls. He was playing the 'Fire Dance' of de Falla, when the telephone rang. Jean picked up the receiver and a female voice asked for Maître.

'No, madame, Mr Rubinstein is not at home.'

'But I can hear him playing the piano.'

'Oh no, madame, it is I who am dusting the keyboard.'

After my father's death I decided to go to New York. In the autumn of 1937, a few months after my arrival, I was asked by the New York Philharmonic Orchestra to conduct a series of concerts at the Lewisohn Stadium the following year. The news surprised me, as I had never dreamed of getting such an opportunity in so short a time. Apparently the Chairman of the Board, in the course of a conversation with Toscanini about musical life in Italy, had asked the Maestro if there were any up and coming young conductors. Toscanini mentioned me as a young man who was doing well in Europe and who had conducted recently at La Scala with success. His words started the ball rolling.

Massimo, in Rome for a concert, was staying in an old-fashioned residential hotel, the Hôtel de Russie, when Leopold Stokowski, giving his name as 'Mr Allen', appeared with a problem. 'A dear friend' of his was arriving from Munich and he had been unable to find lodgings. Could Massimo use his connections with the hotel? Massimo said he'd try, but found that the manager was out. So he suggested that Stokowski bring his friend round the following day, and they'd tackle the problem again.

When I returned to the hotel the following morning it slipped my mind, possibly because I was exhausted after a three-hour rehearsal, that I had told the porter he could let Mr Allen into my suite if he arrived before me. So I was startled, on coming into the sitting-room, to find Stokowski sunk into the sofa with a lady next to him. She wore an outsize raincoat, a broad-brimmed slouch hat over a pair of enormous dark glasses, and flat shoes. I was introduced as 'my dear friend and Maestro', she as 'darling, sweet Miss Gustavson'. The only exposed part of her body was the tip of her nose and a pair of pale lips. Her voice was deep and melodious.

She gave me the shortest possible look and went over to the window to admire the view. Very anxious to solve the problem of their lodgings, I asked the manager to come up. He was a thin little man, with an unhealthy face and dark moustaches that pointed upwards. He dressed in a close-fitting morning coat with a silvery tie. After many years of dealing with foreigners, he could make concessions to several languages, though with a most individual delivery. Stokowski, at his most theatrical, moved the servile creature to such a point that it was agreed that an empty room connected with my suite should be furnished to accommodate my friends. The only snag was that they had to share my bathroom. Stokowski was delighted. He thanked me effusively for my generosity and promised that they would be most unobtrusive and would do everything possible not to distract me. They both knew, he said, being professionals themselves, the demands on an artist when he is performing. Miss Gustavson continued to look out of the window.

I said they must have lunch with me. The manager, puzzled but endlessly accommodating, bowed his way out, and in no time at all a table was being laid in my sitting-room and the head waiter with menus and a wine list was standing by to take our order. Stokowski was enchanted. He took several very deep breaths and launched into a eulogy of Graeco-Roman civilisation.

Miss Gustavson then took off her raincoat and hat. She was wearing a tweed skirt and a loose rollneck jersey that emphasised her pale face and her profile. As the Garbo profile was arguably the most celebrated image in the entire history of the cinema, the 'Miss

Gustavson' persona seemed suddenly a little transparent. It is one thing to be told that the Eiffel Tower is in fact St Pancras Station, but quite another to believe it.

We sat down at the table, the head waiter in attendance. The bill of fare was full of variety and as the others seemed somewhat hesitant, to speed our selection I made a few suggestions. They drew no response. After a while Miss Gustavson decided she would like some salmon, which was at least progress even if salmon was almost the only thing not listed on the menu. The head waiter asked permission to rush to the restaurant to inquire if some salmon could be found, came back breathlessly to report that it could, and some fifteen minutes later reappeared with a silver tray on which was balanced a beautiful fish with parsley sticking out of its mouth. By that stage I would have settled for anything that merely constituted a decision, so when there were cries of admiration I began to believe in myself again as a host. Only for a moment. Miss Gustavson changed her mind. She told me that people ate too much, and that she would rather have some raw carrots, celery and 'those delicious small tomatoes' that tasted so good in the Mediterranean countries. My heart sank. This was 1938, before the Americans had, during the war, started the fashion for eating raw vegetables. At that time in Italy only donkeys were fed on carrots.

Stokowski was easier. He decided on a mutton chop with a green salad and a raspberry syrup with soda. To be courteous, but without enthusiasm, I asked Miss Gustavson if she would like some wine. She told me that French white wine was delicious and good for the health. I proposed a Pouilly Fuissé or Pouilly Fumé, or a dry Chablis 1934.

She asked me if it was really dry. The head waiter confirmed that it was indeed a dry wine. As she seemed a little doubtful he went down to the restaurant again to consult the sommelier. He returned with a broad smile to announce that the vintage was a particularly excellent dry wine. Miss Gustavson then, surprisingly, said she didn't like dry wines and she would rather have, in a jug, a mixture of peaches, pineapple, oranges and any other type of exotic fruit.

At the end of the luncheon I was a spent force. It was late in the afternoon, I had had no rest and my second rehearsal was about to start.

When I got back to the hotel, my principal concern was to avoid meeting them, so I went straight to the restaurant to have a frugal supper in peace before going to bed. When I went upstairs, I opened the sitting-room door cautiously, anxious not to make any noise. There they were, waiting to say goodnight. As we had to share the bathroom there was a protracted charade of artificial politeness: 'Ladies first' – 'Never, you have been working' – 'Oh no, you are my guests' – 'Never, you are the Maestro.' All this took place while we were holding our toothbrushes. We eventually said goodnight and I went to bed in a daze.

Toscanini was seldom happy. I was shocked when he told me once, at the height of his career, 'I have never had a happy day in my life.' I think it was true. He was often displeased with himself. He was always upset by a person's lack of integrity and by an artist indulging in vulgar effects, or not adhering to the composer's intentions. I believe Toscanini's interpretative powers derived not only from intellectual reasoning but from the dramatic emotion tempered by a balanced Latin mind. My wife asked him once in my presence which composer he preferred, Haydn or Mozart. 'Haydn,' he replied, 'there is blood in Haydn.' He then sprang from his chair and fetched the score of Mozart's 'Requiem' which was lying on the piano. 'Look, look,' he almost shouted, 'in the "Tuba Mirum" he scores only one trombone'; and he threw the book on the floor in distress.

Philip Glazebrook

THE ELECTRIC ROCK GARDEN

❧

Philip Glazebrook and David Singh, a Sikh prince, heir to the principality of Faridkot in northern India, became friends at Cambridge in the 1950s. Philip writes: 'It was not until I saw him in India, and had the chance to learn a little about India from my own travels with him and without him, that I understood David's character at all. He threw a light on India for me to see it by, and India threw its light on him. What I learned about both is intended as the subject of this book.'

Philip first visited India in 1973:

It was the variety of the traffic – the collision of eras – which made the Indian highway into a battlefield. Mightiest were the public carriers, trucks top-heavy with passengers which screamed down the middle of the road trumpeting their horns; but there were bicycles too, and bullock-carts carrying bricks and donkey-carts piled with cane, and camels swaying along loaded with iron rods, and road-gangs of women swinging their picks. It was a highway shared by every sort of traffic that ever used a road since the dawn of time. You had to tuck in and swing out, judging the speed of camels going one way and trucks coming another, you had to allow for the waywardness of donkeys and the machismo of humans, you had to accelerate into the twentieth century and brake for the fourteenth. You could have an accident in any century you chose.

The Clark Shiraz, and all Agra, was well crowded with groups who had come, as had I, to see the Taj Mahal and move on rapidly elsewhere. They brought to it, again as I did, not knowledge of what they were to see, but over-familiarity with its appearance. Each of us had seen thousands of representations of the Taj, in paint, in stone, in plastic and in various kinds of wood. Everyone knows what the Taj looks like. Now, if a work of art is to remain one of the wonders of the world, then it must survive all the debasing over-familiarity you carry to its gate and still knock your eyes out when you see it first. The Taj does that. You are filled with the contentment of watching a full moon in a cloudless sky. It is perfect. So refined is its proportion that it has the impact of something immense, so that you start back and look up in wonder, combined with the appeal of the miniature, which makes you want to lean down and peep through its lattices.

That afternoon David took me to the President's tea-party at Rashtrapati Bhavan, Lutyens's Viceregal Lodge, 'whose proportions [the guide book rightly says] are quite unstinting'. The tea too was unstinting, tea outdoors on the grand scale, apotheosis of all the rain-threatened outdoor teas I had eaten with David among the rickety chairs of English orchards. Here was a Moghul garden sharp with the fastidious shapes of clipped trees, straight walks, stone vases, the brightly painted soldier placed on each corner making the whole scene look like a beautifully made board game which someone very grand indeed at the palace windows above us – and he alone – knew how to play. The idea of an electric rock garden came back into my mind. Here any wonder seemed possible.

There were guests in hundreds. There were glossy grand Indians progressing over lawns with their court circling them, there were foreign diplomats in groups, and minor bigwigs, and occasional ragged souls representing Democracy, and a great many more generals than you would think were needed. Through the crowd, behind a bow-wave of aides, rushed Mrs Gandhi in her usual hurry. On his crimson and gilt sofa the portly President nodded among his cushions, representative of the authority hidden in the long stone façade above him, delegate of the hidden power which understood the game. In hollow spaces in the crowd we met acquaintances, sipped tea, chatted with generals. Food was eagerly sought, the attendants' trays soon stripped, like the trees along the highways. Women crowded cakes onto their plates with quick looters' fingers, men ate voraciously, fragments of icing clinging to their moustaches. It was hot, the sun tiring. News kept reaching us by word of mouth that there was a foreign lady, another European, on my track somewhere in the garden; it rather irritated David for some reason, who complained 'It's as if they are wanting to serve this woman up hot for you, like a muffin.' When she appeared I found I knew her, or had known her, long ago in Rome. It was rather a relief to walk off into the garden together; the recognition of kinship with another European made me realise what a comfortable and restorative relationship such kinship is among a foreign race.

David and Philip set off for Faridkot to stay with David's father at his 'shipwrecked ocean liner' of a palace.

January 27. Into Faridkot by night. Iron gates off the town street, scurry of soldiers round the car, a glimpse of peacock-blue palace above. Pulled up under a porte-cochère where we left the car and entered the building by glass doors. Confronted by a heavy rumpled figure in a rust-red cashmere sweater – His Highness. A large stone hall two storeys in height, arches everywhere, stone floor dotted with chairs. Mistakenly I grasped David's grandmother's hand and shook it warmly – it almost came off she was so surprised – while David with a practised swoop touched her feet. Beckoned by HH I sat on a comfortless cane settee between himself and this wordless granny the colour of old ivory. Is the electric rock garden hers? The instant the seat of HH's baggy trousers touched the settee a band struck up behind some archway, where it scraped away on violin and piano until bedtime. Spidery music. Rhythm brushes. Tunes you'd have heard in the Savoy dining-room in the thirties ... HH had thought I was a cavalryman (David telling him so to please him with the *idea* of my coming?) and was childishly disappointed, having looked out several books on cavalry actions for my opinion on tactics. Baulked of military talk he piled the books on my knees rather sulkily, as if I were an impostor, whilst I bowed thanks as best I could without upsetting his mother off the end of the settee.

He renews acquaintance with the old lady the following day at breakfast.

Much earlier than I had stipulated I was summoned to breakfast. In a cluster of servants I found only the old Queen picking disconsolately at her fruit salad whilst trying to manage her shawls so as to keep out icy draughts from stone archways and open doors ... The old lady – she resembles Queen Victoria, except in colour – read to herself several times a letter from Hindustani Motors, causing conversation to languish. She would not move cup or plate as much as an inch herself, waiting for large brown hands to intrude over her shawled shoulder. The number of servants has the same purpose as all the useless space in the guesthouse: to enhance dignity by their presence, not to do necessary work ...

Breakfast over, the Queen proposed a walk in the garden. I wondered if I was to be consulted about the Hindustani Motors communiqué which she brought with her. Away we trailed by stone walks and tubbed flowers. By her passing she gently, momentarily, agitated the crowd of malis into sweeping or weeding, as if a small electric shock was rippling through a somnolent hydra. There was croquet, there was tennis, and, perhaps in deference to Chief Ichalkaranji (who expresses in a book about his visit to England the opinion that 'golf is the chief pastime of the aristocracy'), there was a golf driving net; but I noticed that the mesh of the net was too large to stop a golf ball passing through it, and the croquet hoops were set so near the edge of the lawn that a game on that pitch would have been impossible, even with flamingos for mallets. The *idea* of games was what was provided; nobody wanted to play them. We wound our way between these abstract sports facilities and the small blue summerhouses dotted about the plots of grass, conversation limping along between us. A large many-trunked banyan tree crowds up against the house with the look of an octopus struggling to pull down the stricken liner. Built in 1890 and painted peacock-blue, the house has a wing added in – of all unlikely years to be adding wings to your palace – 1944. I wouldn't have been surprised by an electric rock garden somewhere about. I saw we were circling inside a compound, and would soon regain the terrace from which we had set out.

'Do you have a rock garden, Highness?'

A gently superior smile. 'The palace garden area is amounting to almost sixteen acres all told.'

A few days after returning from Faridkot Philip flew on his own to Madras, heading on to the ashram of Sri Aurobindo in Pondicherry.

I had not sat pondering very long on my bed in that oubliette of a room before Mr Goyle, fragment of the Universal Mind, came stealing in. He was the manager of the establishment. Neat of hair, earnest, short, with a mild glow of conviction lighting up his eyes behind his spectacles, he managed far more than the mere outward needs of his guests, food and rest, for he was tuned to another wavelength, a prison governor listening to his captives' inmost secrets by means of bugged cells, and in consequence he moved about the house guided and informed by whispers of the Higher Wisdom in his ear. He wore a white shirt and a dhoti, and a rare smile showed brown teeth. What you noticed at once about his presence was the calm: it was like a sedative, and he went round the rooms under his care issuing himself in opiate form to excitable guests. I noticed too, as he glided about, that his hands were very large in proportion to his body, like the Buddha's. We talked, friends at once. He knew the hesitation of my nature, the uncertainty of my mind. No doubt they were commonplace in beached wanderers found on the ashram's shore …

His outlook was assured and simple. He knew the truth: what he knew was true … Because he had done more reading than thinking his head was full, not quite of ideas, but of maxims gleaned from Aurobindo's writings, which served him for bridges over any little difficulties the world of actual experience might present. 'Nature chisels and moulds, so there has to be pain.' 'The seer looks at pain and laughs.' That's the problem of pain dealt with. Our wandering conversation touched too, as is inevitable between a European and an Indian who resents that India's early magnificence is unknown to Europeans, on the culture and omniscience of prehistoric India. But nothing is known of it, I said. Seas of butter. He smiled (he was an exceptionally good-tempered man): television, airplanes, they had invented them all in early days beside the Indus, and had allowed them to lapse because of their triviality compared with the search for wisdom. Why, I asked, had archaeologists never come on traces of these things? Because, he replied, an archaeologist cannot discover the remains of a technology his own era isn't familiar with – how could a nineteenth-century excavator recognise the remains of a television set? – so all India's earlier wizardry had been shovelled onto the spoil-heap by ignorant Westerners.

When he left me – concerned equally with catering and First Causes he had business in the kitchen – I found that I liked and respected him. I should have expected to feel irritated by his want of rigour, exasperated by his non sequitur mind, glad to see the back of him. Instead, with rather the same surprise as I had felt in liking His Highness at Faridkot, I found I rather admired Mr Goyle.

Leaving the ashram, Philip takes the bus to Bangalore.

There were about seventy people aboard the bus, crushed together like the crowd in a rush-hour tube. It was a social mix. No doubt the poorest class wasn't present, though a more or less naked beggar sat next to me for one stage and nudged me and poked me with that whispering persistence which will harden the most charitable heart. At another time there was an ugly bourgeois gent in a brown suit on board, evidently proud of his English, who put me through an interrogation shouted from the other end of the bus. Everyone listened, watching me with placid brown eyes which were without either animosity or sympathy. The beggar saw me as a mark, the babu saw me as a means of showing off, the youth beside me saw me as a headrest; but none of them showed a scrap of interest in the foreigner amongst them.

Then by train to Mysore.

Cocooned in comfortable notions I strolled about Mysore enjoying the statues under stone canopies, the Jubilee clocks, the pillared façades of town hall and hospital and university, and the dust raised in the sunlight by ambling bullock-carts and trotting rickshaws. It was a curious mixture, princely Mysore. There was the rubbish of Indian towns, but an unusual municipal wish for the rubbish not to be there, a wish expressed in dustbins standing on mounds of garbage. On their sides was printed 'Use Me', and inside them, using them indeed, the dogs fought for scraps.

The 'top hole accommodation on the Poona Mail', promised by the booking-clerk, proved an illusion. And dismounting at Londa, 'a wayside junction in the midst of a hill-forest', Philip found himself 'outside anyone's care'.

The next train onwards to Panjim was due at 3.30 am, ten hours away. I put my luggage in the lockable cloakroom cupboard (the ticket issued by the station master for this service managed to incorporate 400 words of bureaucratese) and walked in the setting sun up and down the platform, which ended each way in jungle. The sun sank; the rails glittered and went out. I retired to the first-class waiting-room and read the notices on the walls. There were three. The first said 'Hot Water Supplied on Request. Fee 8 annas for 3 buckets. Apply Station Master.' A second said 'Walls whitewashed 8.12.72.' But it was the third that made me ponder, a pregnant yet tentative statement which might have been formulated by Sri Aurobindo himself: 'Trains Running Late Are Liable to Make Up or Lose Some Time.' It was the sort of statement Mr Goyle would have been happy with.

Grizel Hartley

GRIZEL
GRIZEL HARTLEY REMEMBERED

edited by P. S. H. Lawrence

❧

I published this book for a group of Grizel Hartley's friends in 1991. Married to an Eton master, she had been a colourful and amusing figure, with a great capacity to inspire and bestow affection. Obviously acquaintance with Grizel herself would be a prerequisite for catching the spirit of the book's contents; but there are pleasing moments for a wider audience. Her husband, Hubert Hartley, retired in 1957 and started working in London with a shipping firm, and she did some teaching for a while at a girls' public school The book contains a selection of her letters written between 1935 and 1987, her commonplace book and an afterword by her cousin Janet Adam Smith.

To Richard Ollard, 25 October 1953.

At Taplow I emerged into swirling white mist and a feeling of loose horses in the air, and one car, to which I said 'Are you a taxi?'

It replied 'I'm Mr Talbot.'

It took me home, and I said 'How did you know where I lived,' and it replied, in the manner of one who identifies himself with the Deity

'I'm Mr Talbot.'

To John Verney, 21 September 1979.

This is one from Wilfrid Blunt you may have heard.

'How do you like your coffee?'
'May I have it without cream?'
'I'm afraid we haven't any cream, would you like it without milk?'

To John Wilkes, 28 March 1983.

I am relieved that even you and Joanie find some words difficult in the 'Times' Crossword, and not all in my dictionary, which is the lovely one, Chambers, where an éclair is 'a cake, long in shape but short in duration'. I like it better than the O.E.D.

A mathematical trick, taken from one of her letters.

You write down any 3 digit number, such as 971 (any number as long as the difference between the first and last figure is 2 or more than 2).

So	971
Then write it in reverse	179
Subtract the smaller from the larger	792
Turn the answer round	297
And add it up, and it comes to	1089

Whatever figures you choose, the answer will always be 1089. I can't think why.

Roger Hinks

THE GYMNASIUM OF THE MIND
THE JOURNALS OF ROGER HINKS
1933–1963

edited by John Goldsmith

❧

James Lees-Milne writes in 'Holy Dread', the ninth volume of his Diaries: 'I have been sent my copy of Roger Hinks's diaries ... I was one of the sponsors. Dozens of publishers refused to take it. It is chock-a-block with wisdom and intellectual speculation about art and life, a wonderful book. I wish the whole diary could have been published instead of snippets. What a reflection on publishers and the reading public that this extremely serious work could only be printed twenty years after the author's death after a handful of friends had guaranteed it.'

There's an issue here – the issue of subsidised publication. Obviously the business arrangements between publisher and individual author must be confidential, but I have no anxiety about accepting funding, on occasion, for creditable but possibly uncommercial ventures. My criterion, which sounds too smug for words, is that I don't want to put my imprint on what I think is a rotten book, regardless of the financial inducements. It seems to me bad business, and I cannot reconcile myself to the idea that an author's vanity is somehow being served if his meagre and reluctant audience are groaning at his lack of talent; though I suppose they never tell him.

Having had access to the whole diary, I'd disagree with Lees-Milne about publishing the whole thing (in more volumes). Patrick Leigh Fermor, in his admirable – even by his standards – Portrait Memoir, refers to the diaries talking 'with some freedom of heterodox affections', but in some of the unpublished parts they go a little further than that. I thought John Goldsmith did an excellent job with the editing. He writes in his Editor's Introduction: 'There are at least five different kinds of book that could be made out of the material available; and for each choice of direction there are conflicting clues as to what RH would have himself approved.' What John Goldsmith achieved is a harmonious balance between the artistic meditation and the sharply observed day-to-day activities, to produce a serious but still very accessible whole.

5 September 1935, Berlin. Helene von Nostitz[-Wallwitz] dined with me at the Esplanade this evening. Before dinner we saw André Germain in the hall with a French poet and a handsome young Nazi – two protégés from that curious menagerie of his. The French poet was like all French poets – small, swarthy, restless, and cross: he obviously hated Berlin and André Germain and the Nazi; and derived a good deal of positive satisfaction from hating them. He was dressed in uncompromising black and had a curious green stone in a narrow platinum setting on the little finger of his left hand: he kept nervously twiddling it round, so that one expected him to appear and disappear intermittently; but he sat there silently and malignantly, wishing us at the bottom of the sea. The Nazi boy was tall and broad-shouldered, with cold blue eyes and square ugly peasant hands. He stood at attention and gazed inquiringly at André Germain and Helene and me, switching his cold blue gaze automatically on to whichever of us was speaking, but never saying a word. He was respectful towards Helene, slightly supercilious towards André Germain, and frankly mystified by an Englishman who could speak German easily.

I did not care for either youth, but I could believe that the Nazi was a real character, whereas the Frenchman was a mere literary projection.

24 May 1937, London. I had a letter from a lady at Ipswich beginning thus: 'Dear Sir, I am writing an article on Venus and I should like to know whether he correct name was Venus de Medici or Venus

de Milo. I find the authorities differ on this point ...' I was tempted to reply: 'Dear Madam, Venus was born a Mlle. Anadyomene: she married M. de Medici, and was divorced; she then married en secondes noces M. de Milo who treated her so badly that he broke off both her arms. Yours faithfully ...' But unfortunately civil servants sometimes have consciences.

9 June 1937, London. I believe that friendships were never meant to be eternal, and should be allowed to languish and decay and disappear when they have served their turn. It is the highest compliment one can pay one's friends to treat them with perfect sincerity; and this requires one to abandon them without rancour and without regret when one has nothing more to give them or receive from them ... Friendships are much too precious to be mismanaged and neglected; they ought to be cultivated for all they are worth or avoided altogether ... I feel about loyalty as Dr Johnson felt about patriotism: that it is the last refuge – not perhaps of a scoundrel; but at any rate of a sentimentalist.

23 June 1943, Stockholm. The secret of a reasonable middle age is the elimination of the unnecessary. Fortunately, I have always been good at dispersing what did not concern me: the only difference is that one finds these renunciations natural at forty, whereas at thirty they struck one's friends (though not oneself) as premature.

On a visit to Bernard Berenson at I Tatti in April 1946:

From history we passed by imperceptible degrees to religion. I remarked that one of the unexpected consequences of coming to live in Rome was that I had become strongly anticlerical. Just as many people who come to Rome develop a kind of Catholic attitude by contagious example, without believing a single article of the Catholic faith, I have developed a sort of allergy towards the Vatican and all its works. 'In other words,' said BB, 'you are kicking against Peter and Paul. What harm they have done to Christianity, that cunning pair of propagandists: I have always hated them for it. All the racketeering element in the Church comes from that precious couple. What a beautiful religion it could have been, if they hadn't perverted it ...' Yes, I agreed; yet I suppose but for those two we should never have heard of it.

3 June 1946, Rome. Margaret Bottrall, who has been obliged to go to the North for a few days, asked me to preside over her poetry group on Thursday, and imposed on me the task of dealing with Eliot. After the first shock, the natural recoil from a problem I am so little capable of solving efficiently for her, I am, however, beginning to wonder whether this task is not a blessing in disguise. At any rate, it made me spend the whole of a hot Sunday at home, quietly reading through Tom's entire poetic output – an effort which I could not otherwise have given myself unprompted. In reading text and commentaries with intent, I notice, what had never struck me previously, the two curves – of experience and technique – and their intersection, somewhere about 'Ash Wednesday' (1930): the curve of experience falling away (as it seems to me) with his 'conversion' (which I am bound to put in inverted commas, so unconvincing do I find it), while the curve of technique climbs and climbs, to still more exquisite phrasing, still more perfect ambivalences of sound and sense ... The words in a poem are, after all, a kind of lattice to which the flowers of the imagination cling, and through which (by refocusing of the inward eye) vistas of allusion are perceived, faint and far off, framed in a phrase. All poetry is meant to be read between the lines, but it is only by attending most carefully to the structure of the lines themselves that we can estimate the size and shape and content of the spaces between them.

19 July 1946, Rome. A large dinner-party at the Villa Medici in honour of Jean-Paul Sartre. We were invited for nine; at a quarter to ten we were still standing about in the open portico looking on to the garden, talking desultorily – in my case to Princess Doria and Jacques Veysset: a short cut to schizophrenia, as he is impenitently

worldly and she is exclusively preoccupied with good works. Finally, just as I thought my skull was about to split, like the pomegranate in Valéry's poem, the great man appeared, chaperoned by his Egeria, Mme Simone de Beauvoir, whom the irreverent in Paris call 'La Grande Sartreuse', and by Carlo Levi who, notwithstanding his best seller ['Christ Stopped at Eboli'], appears unable to afford a tie.

From my place at dinner ... I could observe Sartre at ease across the table. The most noticeable thing about him is the cast in his eye: to this I am inclined to attribute his tortuous philosophy – with such a crippling obliquity of vision one cannot but be conscious of the mutual interdependence of l'Etre and le Néant.

I had a little conversation with him in the library after dinner ... I said I was interested in the mechanics of composition and inquired about his technical methods. It seems that Sartre works over and over again on his original manuscript, but that once it is typed he cannot touch it – it lies in a sort of purgatory between the inferno of creation and the paradise of print. I can understand this very well: a typescript is in any case an ugly thing, with a sort of false finality about it, and yet not truly definite. It was a curious lapse from sensibility on Proust's part that the sight of a typescript, or even a galley proof, always excited him to further and further efforts of revision, and even composition.

1 March 1948, Rome. Gore Vidal, a young American novelist, ... is staying at the Eden and we lunched together today ... GV was not shy: which I always find rather agreeable. 'What would you say the colour of my hair was?' he inquired. 'The colour of stale marron glacé,' I replied, feeling that I might as well say what I really thought. 'Yes, but in the summer it's straw blonde,' he rejoined, adding ' – and my body gets the colour of old mahogany: it's sensational ...'

An encounter with the novelist Ivy Compton-Burnett in the summer of 1956.

I saw Ivy at dinner with Madge [Garland] in London the other evening ... We were talking about Angus Wilson's 'Anglo-Saxon Attitudes'. Madge said: 'I hear he wrote it in four months, between two and four in the afternoon.' 'Oh?' said Ivy; 'I can't imagine anyone doing anything between two and four in the afternoon – except hoping that tea would be at four rather than five.' That is the authentic Ivy note; and when people complain that Ivy's characters don't talk like real people, I can only say 'Well, Ivy talks like that.' And she does, in that prim dry voice of hers, neatly depositing those ferocious sentences of hers, as though she were setting a poisoned Madeira cake on an unsuspecting tea table ...

It is the peculiar quality of the talk that gives Ivy's novels their unmistakable flavour. Like the dialogue of Congreve's plays it is extremely stylized. There is no attempt to imitate the inflexions and the rhythms of actual speech, the 'ums' and 'ers' and 'I means' with which we pad the empty corners of our conversation while our minds are panting to catch up with our tongues. Even the permissible 'ohs' and 'wells' are reduced to the bare minimum. In fact, all the complex back-and-forth, the false starts, the broken phrases, the circumlocutions and repetitions of real talk are reduced, refined, clarified, and simplified into short sentences separated by full stops. When we were calculating how many words Angus wrote an hour, on the basis of 'four months every day, two to four,' someone said: 'Ivy, how many words an hour do you write?' 'Ten,' replied Ivy, succinctly. I can easily believe it.

After 1955 Roger Hinks abandoned the diary form and took to writing what he called 'Panjandrums'. Here was the 'gymnasium in which he could exercise his intellectual muscles'. His appointment as British Council Representative in Greece that year was infelicitous – he resented what he saw as the cultural poverty of Greece; the summer heat exhausted him.

Greeks are not literary, in the strict sense, as the English, the French, and the Germans are. Books play a very small part in their lives. They are instinctive bards, rhapsodes, debaters. Thus their language has never settled down in modern times into a fixed grammatical form or acquired a canonical orthography. This exasperates those who, like myself, can learn a language only by its declensions and conjugations and paradigms, who are sticklers for correct usage, who detest the labile and the indeterminate, who cannot work without a row of dictionaries in hand.

Alas, poor Doric. Certainly a couple that he describes in Salonica in January 1957 weren't the social equivalent of canonical orthography.

The mention of decayed gentlewomen reminds me that Mme X and Mlle Y were at their usual table at luncheon today, and welcomed me to Salonica with shrill cries of delight. Whenever I see them I realize how deep an impression Levantine ladies made upon the fancy of Edward Lear: scroobious is the very word for Mlle Y, and nothing could be more ombliferous than the appearance of Mme X; and I can see them all too clearly at the head of limericks beginning: 'There was an old dame from the Bosphorus who damaged her eyebrows with phosphorus ...' and: 'There was an old maid of Salonica who played on a jewelled harmonica ...' They have lived for years in one room at a hotel which is at least a grade below the Ritz; but this is not such a hardship to them, Laz explained, as it would be to me – or indeed to him. 'No, I suppose they can always gossip as they lie in bed in the morning,' I surmised. 'Oh, I don't think they talk to each other much,' Laz put me right. 'They watch each other ... It would not do if Mme X did not know when Mlle Y came in: you see, she is the little one, and the gay one.' I saw. 'Yes, they lie in bed very late in the morning, and it takes them a very long time to dress – at least two hours for Mme X, because there is so much to be done to her face, you see.' Indeed I do – repairing the eyebrows damaged with phosphorus, for instance. And they have to take turns in the bathroom, I imagine? Laz looked rather doubtful: 'Mme X only takes showers, standing up. She tells me that she does not care to sit down in a bath which is used by other people.' No, of course ... and Mlle Y? 'Ah, I don't know about Mlle Y's bath arrangements. But they are certainly both very clean ladies.' And then? 'Well, then it is lunch time, and they go to the restaurant, as you saw.' Every day? 'No, I think they are sometimes elsewhere at lunch.' And then? 'Then Mlle Y gives lessons, and Mme X writes.' About what? 'Love, of course.' And has Mme X great experience in love matters? 'Not so much as Mlle Y.' Ah, no, of course, she is the gay one. 'Yes, and they say she has it with both sexes. They say she is interested in pretty Mrs Z.' Good heavens, is that why the Zs now live in Athens? 'Not only – there is business too.' And is there quite a large Lesbian set in Salonica, apart from the lady doctor and the lady dentist you told me about before? 'Oh yes, of course, there is a lady footballer.'

John McManners

FUSILIER
RECOLLECTIONS AND REFLECTIONS
1939–1945

❧

The author is a distinguished academic, a Fellow of All Souls, who was Professor of History in the universities of Tasmania, Sydney and Leicester before becoming Regius Professor of Ecclesiastical History at Oxford. His account is both robust and perceptive; the subtitle speaks of both recollection and reflection and it's the balance of the two, from someone of real intellect, that makes the book work so well.

When the war came in 1939 he was living in Co. Durham and had just successfully completed his Oxford finals.

My father had been a miner and my mother a schoolteacher; she converted him to Christian belief and coached him through the years of study required to be ordained. All their savings had gone into paying for him to take a year at a theological college. This background of limited means unfortified by inherited possessions, matched to a working-class down-to-earth practicality and ingenuity, made the vicarage unlike most of its contemporaries, which had an air of gentility and scholarly reserve. Ours, in a knockabout fashion, was more comfortable and more interesting to live in.

Commissioned into the Northumberland Fusiliers (he is good on the tensions between the career officers and the enlisted 'amateurs'), he was posted to North Africa. Here is his first encounter with the realities of action.

War is about killing. This is the elementary reality, so obvious as never to need stating, but impossible to accept as part of one's individual thinking until the decisive moment of experience. While we were hanging round dejectedly on flat, endless desert under an iron-grey sky, trucks all packed and ready to move as the sound of firing drew nearer, I was sent on my first reconnaissance. Together with an Australian infantry captain I was to go to a speck on the far skyline to find out what was there, and was there any sign of the enemy? The captain's truck took us part of the way – this was somewhere just west of the road running southwards out of Tobruk to El Adem. I was a complete novice, and he was hardly battle-hardened. Between us, we had neither map nor binoculars. Cluelessly we set off together to have a look, in the Arabic-inspired jargon of Eighth Army, 'have a *shufti*': no orderlies with us, no one to cover us, and walking upright. The feature turned out to be a sandbagged post, and on realising this we started crawling. When we looked over the parapet there were about a dozen dead Germans, slashed to bits with grenade fragments and bayonet thrusts. That night, I took out one of my few Forces letter forms and wrote to John Brewis, my old tutor at Oxford and now Principal of St Chad's theological college at Durham, near home. It was to say that, if I ever got back, I intended to be ordained and I wanted him to remind me.

On the 'Great Retreat' (from Tobruk):

On the morning of the next day I could see something out of the ordinary on a solitary hillock on the skyline. Leaving the water truck behind I drove forward observing through binoculars. It was a truck, with a flag raised. Nearer still and it was a huge Union Jack. There was an officer there waiting to direct the lost. 'Northumberland Fusiliers: Major Hamilton of your lot passed here a couple of hours ago, you'll probably catch him' – and he gave me a compass bearing. So we did, finding Tommy and his driver sitting disconsolately at the side of their pickup truck having a lunch of bully and army biscuits. The NAAFI loot provided them with dessert and my party with both courses. Tommy's adventures had resembled mine, and like me he had got through because he had been going first – it is all or nothing when you are leading: either you get shot and those behind get the chance to flee, or you slip through and those behind are caught. I was full of euphoria at having escaped, but Tommy was haunted by the loss of the entire company, his first command. 'Where do you suppose we'll report?' he asked. 'Sidi Bishr,' I replied, 'it's where we always go after a defeat and where all the girl friends know where to find us.' We hit the coast road and went on to Alexandria. There was traffic both ways, battered, dusty travellers (though by now only a few) going back to what passed for civilisation, smart and grim-looking troops going west towards the last line of defence at Alamein. As we drove through the slums of Alex the hostility of the locals was evident, like an evil miasma in the air. There were some jeers, some thumbs down and something else they had learnt from us, the V sign of contempt, not V for victory but derision with upward jabbing motions. They were looking forward to looting our camps (considering their misery, could one blame them?) and to getting new profits from the advancing Germans. But no one dared to proceed to hostile acts. We were a downcast defeated lot, but armed and easily provoked.

His closing note:

Adventuring round the world has its satisfactions, even long term, for one has memories and, perhaps to the exasperation of friends, anecdotes. But I am sure that complete happiness is found only in the quiet oases of life, the little worlds of friendship and concern where you are understood, and understand. Life in the vicarage, with the parish comings and goings giving it purpose and flavour, was such a refuge, and one hoped, in turn, to build another family unit to the exclusion of the harshness of the too-busy world, and to exorcise the contrary curse of loneliness. And now, for me, there was Oxford, more and more during the years becoming my social and spiritual home. After six years I was visiting it again with a new, overriding certainty that this was not only the milieu which had moulded me and transformed me, but also the place above all others where happiness was to be found. I was to rejoin it and then to venture away again deliberately, for what can they know of Oxford who only Oxford know? But God has brought me here again. It is good to have done one's best work here, and it is good, when work is over, to look forward to dying here.

The study of theology, as an intellectual discipline, was fascinating, enjoyable. It meant so much more to me than it had before, as its conundrum aspects receded. Since that day in Tobruk I had thought through and rationalised the impact of the sudden sight of those slaughtered Germans; what had happened was that Christian belief had become intensely personal. Up to then I had followed, in intellectual debates, the *via eminentia* of Christian apologetics: the order and beauty of creation, the working of laws in the universe, spiritual experience, show there must be a God. Then, look around for signs of God's activity in the moral sphere, and we find the story of a good man preaching and healing in Palestine; he is crucified, his followers worship him – but the sight of the dead bodies in the sandbagged post at Tobruk ended that chain of argument. I had seen what men out of their God-given freedom do to each other. This was the face of evil, and I was part of the evil, being glad, even in revulsion, that they were dead. People tell academics and clergy to look at what the 'real world' is like. By this they mean dictating letters, selling and buying shares, instituting manufacturing processes, tapping information into computers. But behind their world is the real world they have forgotten: the battlefield. Here is the ultimate reason of the social order written in letters of lead and shards of steel. In face of this, you cannot believe in God, the God of the deists. But you can, almost in despair, turn to the God who suffers with his creation, accepting the burden of sin that arises from human freedom, and taking it on himself. Religious apologetics begin from Jesus on the cross: the Christian life is allegiance to him.

But it still did not follow that I had to be ordained. I attended chapel every morning and, as far as university affairs allowed, every evening, hoping for the guidance that never came. I was lucky in having as my personal tutor Michael Ramsay, who had just married Joan Hamilton, sister of my old ally Tommy of the Northumberland Fusiliers. Their friendship, and that of Stanley Greenslade, the other canon-professor, and the background influence of my father (a determined Christian believer in a very different intellectual sphere) drew me towards the ministry of the Church in which they all served. We know now, as was not known then, what enervating effects war can have on the minds of combatants: having made life and death decisions and being haunted by them, they lose the capacity for deciding. In fact, there is a sense in which you can never know for sure beforehand if a vocational decision is the right one; until you accept the duties you cannot know they were meant for you – a dilemma which forces a gamble. Ordination, I kept telling myself, meant total allegiance, the willingness to do anything and go anywhere, something I could not feel then and never have felt. Yet I was unable to move off, apply for an academic job in history or a course in law leading to the Bar – there was a constraint defying logical argument.

Half-way through the course of theology at Durham John Kelly wrote to me – my old college at Oxford invited me back as chaplain after I had done a year in a parish. So I was ordained just like the port-filled dons of old, to go to a Fellowship. Would I have done so if the invitation had not come? I could not say then and I still do not know.

Neil Macvicar

A HEART'S ODYSSEY

❧

Neil Macvicar was born and brought up in Scotland. A QC, he was appointed to the Bench as a sheriff in Edinburgh and served for seventeen years. He had been a classical scholar at Oriel College, Oxford when the Second World War started and he joined the Army. After service in Tunisia and Italy as a young Gunner officer, he went to Greece in 1944, when the British Army intervened in the outbreak of the Greek civil war. He felt an immediate affinity with the Greek people, and in return Greece brought him some odd adventures, friendship and, before long, love. It's a well written, attractive book, with a good title. The Prologue gives it its heart.

Marily and I were married at the Saint – *ston Ayio,* as they say in Corfu. They mean, of course, in the church behind the Plateia, with the tall red-nightcapped bell tower, where their patron saint, Spyridion, lies in his silver casket and embroidered slippers, serenely awaiting the Last Trump.

It was the inevitable place for our wedding, given that the saint is almost one of Marily's family. His mortal remains (less one forearm, which had at one time been detached and was venerated in a church in Rome) came into it along with the sheets and pillow-cases and silver spoons of a dowry, and were cared for by a succession of family priests for four hundred years. By the time that I arrived in Corfu, rights of private property in a sacred relic had become unacceptable, and Saint Spyridion had been de-privatised. But Marily's grandfather, Papa Stephanos, still remained the priest of the church, and our nuptials would have been incomplete without the old miracle-worker to give us his blessing from his shrine behind the marble *iconostasis.*

He must have been the only cool person present. It was the hottest day of a hot Greek summer. At six in the evening the high houses and narrow streets of the town were beginning to give back the heat that the sun had poured into them since dawn. In the oasis of the church the temperature was only relatively more bearable. Beneath the painted saints and angels on the ceiling and the hanging silver lamps and candelabra, the congregation was a-flutter with handkerchiefs and fans. Sweating in my kilt, with full rig of dress jacket and lace jabot, I began to think that the desire to create a romantic Scottish-Hellenic effect had been too much of a good thing.

The service was conducted not by Papa Stephanos, but by the bishop's *protosyngelos*, the Archimandrite Chrysanthos. He was very fat and imposing and might, I suspect, have become a bishop himself if he had not suffered from the defect, serious in an Orthodox cleric, of not being able to sing in tune. The ceremony floated with Byzantine deliberation on the current of his monotone. The betrothal rings were placed on our fingers; the ribbon-linked wreaths of orange blossom were passed and re-passed above, and finally settled on, our heads; together we drank blessed wine from the marriage cup. At one point the lovely guileless girl at my side stood smartly and without any warning on my toes, to let me know, according to an old Greek custom, which of us was to be the boss. Lastly, the *protosyngelos*, his beard foaming over the prow of his stomach, led us thrice round the table in Isaiah's dance, through a blatter of rice and rose petals.

It was a long way from my douce, Piskie, Edinburgh beginnings, but such is the spell of love that it all seemed most marvellously foreordained. Pure chance, reason says, that I was a subaltern in a regiment which happened to be handy in the south of Italy in December 1944, and could de diverted to war-riven Athens. Yet even now the solemnities at the Saint feel as if they were both the start of a new journey and the destined culmination of an old one, on which I had set out before I was aware of it.

Greeks have never struck me as conspicuously pious. Most of them, even forty years ago when their society was less secular and material than it is today, sat lightly to their religion. The Orthodox Church was respected for the lead it had always given in resistance to foreign oppression ... , but the attitude towards individual priests tended to be one of amused tolerance. In Corfu they are supposed to bring bad luck. (The traditional method for a man to avert this, on meeting a priest, is to touch his trousers discreetly in the region of his private parts.)

His own, presumably, not the priest's.

We are introduced to the elder members of Marily's family in Corfu. Maria is Marily's 'Nono', grandmother, one of whose sisters, Silvia, deserted by her sea captain husband, spent the remaining forty-five years of her life first with Maria, then with Marily's father, Spiro.

She, too, must have been a lovely girl, but she had not worn so well as Maria, and was, when I first knew her, already becoming reclusive and a little odd. Her letters were almost impossible to read, being written in Greek transliterated into Roman script, in a spidery sloping hand, and complicated by her old-fashioned paper-saving trick of writing twice over the same side of the sheet, the second time at right angles to the first.

Aunt Lydia, the third sister, had also made a childless marriage which ended in divorce. She lived alone on a family property at the village of Viro, a thin, ill-looking, unhappy woman who, it was said, drank too much. Bits of the property had been sold, little by little, to pay debts and she was left with the small, charming, but decrepit house, a tangle of gardens and a grove of trees producing the finest oranges in the world.

There was a whiff of defeat in the air and none of the family felt the departure of ancestral glory more sharply than Marily's father, Spiro Bulgari. He had an almost incestuous affection for his native island, so strong that he never, if he could help it, set foot outside it, even to the mainland opposite. But it was more truly a nostalgia for the Corfu of the Venetians and for the aristocratic principle. Since the end of the 'Enetokratia' [1797] everything had been gradually going downhill. The British had, for a while, stopped the rot, confirming the old families in their privileges and even making some of their members Knights of the Most Noble Order of St Michael and St George. But the Greeks of the modern state seemed to him irredeemably vulgar ...

He was not much more polite about the ordinary people of the island. A race 'senza fede' he described them – without faith, not to be trusted. And indeed the Corfiots had a traditional reputation for treachery and the stiletto. They certainly tend to use charm as a substitute for reliability. 'We are all terrible liars, you know,' they say with a disarming smile and offer you a drink, or a basket of mulberries, to compensate you for having let you down for the third time. One might almost be in the Outer Hebrides, except for the weather.

I may be making my father-in-law sound like a sour and snobbish fainéant, but in fact his nature was at odds with his attitudes. He was, when I first met him, an active and highly intelligent man of forty-three – though not as intellectually inclined as his father. He held for many years the post of administrative director of the Corfu Psychiatreion, which he ran so well that it had the reputation of being one of the best in Greece. This was not simply a tribute to his efficiency. He showed a genuine affection for the unfortunates under his care and generated a spirit of calm and goodwill which made up for the hospital's shortcomings in modern facilities.

The old madhouse still stands where it did, beside the main road that runs southward out of town from Sarocco Square. A garden with high railings adjoins the road, under whose eucalyptus trees the less disturbed residents shamble about for most of the day, occasionally begging a cigarette or a drachma from passers-by. This can only be therapeutic for those outside as well as in. One defective called Taso was well known to the community, because he was allowed to carry a banner in the saint's processions. These outings, four times a year, were all that Taso lived for. Clad in a voluminous blue cassock, he lumbered, splay-footed, bearing aloft the banner of the Panayia on an enormous pole and exchanging grins and garbled greetings with friends in the crowd. His sense of location being poor, he sometimes wandered from his proper place in the procession, causing disruption in the ranks of brass bands and cohorts of marching high school girls; but any threats to bar him from taking part so upset Taso that the Director preferred to risk official displeasure rather than the suicide of one of his patients.

One warms to Leni, one of the village community.

In a house looking on to the back courtyard lived Leonidas and Leni, the more-or-less honorary guardians of the property. Leonidas was a skilful gardener and olive cultivator, but fonder of ouzo than hard work. Leni was industrious, unassuming and one of the best-hearted women one could hope to meet. She was illiterate and had a local reputation as a simpleton. We all, I regret, made merry that she had mistaken her husband's directions and put into the ballot box, instead of her voting paper, their electricity bill.

William Magan

MIDDLE EASTERN APPROACHES
EXPERIENCES AND TRAVELS OF AN INTELLIGENCE OFFICER 1939–1948

❧

At the beginning of the Second World War Bill Magan, a serving officer in the Indian Cavalry, was assigned to the Intelligence Bureau in Delhi. It proved to be a permanent deflection in his military career and he spent the war years in Intelligence, travelling extensively in the Middle East, and worked thereafter in MI5. He could speak Persian, having spent a year in Shiraz some years before. The following encounter took place in Persia in 1942.

I stopped the night at a little pub, a replica, I imagine, of a thousand other little pubs between this and Moscow. A little door led in from the street and, behind windows stocked with bottles of vodka, wines and beer, was the parlour, furnished with bare wooden benches and tables spread with Persian carpets. In one corner was a radio. Across the passage was the kitchen where servants in their shirt-sleeves were busy at a huge oven under which blazed a fire of logs. Two or three men with no apparent purpose sat about in the kitchen smoking their long 'chapooks' and drinking tea out of little glasses known as 'finjans'. Behind, and down a few steps, were three guest rooms leading off a passage, the last of which was assigned to me.

I was so covered with fine dust that I looked like a miller. There were no washing facilities in the pub, so I took an escort, a bootblack, who plied his trade outside the door of the pub and was ready to earn a few krans any way he could, and went to the local 'hamam', or public bath. It was a noisome place, but I got a cubicle to myself with a shower in it. There were two taps labelled 'hot' and 'cold', but both produced rather smelly scalding water, and I managed with some difficulty to clean myself, listening as I did so to the slappings and gurglings of the faithful enjoying to the full all the delights to which the Persian bath attendant subjects his customers. There was also in my cubicle an elegant and almost poetical notice written with that economy of language which so distinguishes the best Persian style, and in a calligraphy which was truly artistic, telling customers to be careful of their valuables for the management could take no responsibility for losses. It was so brief and striking that I committed it to memory.

While I was supping off a tender chicken, a bowl of greasy soup and some salad, the man of all works, corresponding to the 'butler' in an Irish hotel, came in and said, 'Berlin is finished. Wiped off the map.' 'That's good,' I replied, 'who managed that feat?' 'The Russians. It's completely wiped from the face of the earth. What's more, the Germans are in full retreat.' 'Splendid!' I said. 'Where are they retreating?' 'All along the whole front' was his reply. 'The Germans are utterly finished.' He had got the news, he said, from a friend who had heard it on the radio. So, with those comforting tidings, I picked the bones of my chicken dry, leaving just enough to interest the half dozen or so cats which had appeared through my window and had been mobbing me ever since my supper had arrived.

After supper, I sat in the courtyard for a bit in the cool fresh air of the evening, and then went to bed. I slept for a little, but a swarm of sandflies, and the ever-increasing noise in the bar as the guests grew merrier, and the blaring of oriental music on the radio, soon had me awake again. At about half past eleven there came a knocking on my door. I said nothing, as I thought it might be another guest wanting to share my room, and I hoped he would get sick of knocking and go away. But the knocking grew more persistent, so I shouted in a sleepy voice, 'Go away. What do you want?' The man of all works replied, 'The Russians have come, and they want to see your passport.' I said, 'Tell them that this is no time of night to come waking me up, so they can go away and come back in the morning.'

There was some mumbling, and then the voice began again. 'They say they must see your passport now, and also that you must move your car out of the street.'

'Tell them I am a British officer, and they can see my papers in the morning, and that I am damned if I am going to move my car, as it's not in anyone's way and I have to start early in the morning.'

There was more mumbling, and then, 'They say they must see your papers and they won't go away till they have done so.'

'Very well then, bring them in.'

'But I can't get in. I've been trying for the last ten minutes and the door is locked.'

'It isn't locked, you ass. Open it!'

He opened it and came in followed by two Russians. The officer was a nice clean-looking little man with a long, sad moustache. His orderly was a huge man with a Mongoloid face. They both saluted, and I sat up in bed.

The officer talked to the waiter in Russian, and he translated into Persian.

'He says, who are you?'

'Tell him I am a British officer coming from the British Legation in Teheran and carrying official mail for the British Consul-General in Meshed.'

Some mumbling in Russian. The Russian officer took out his notebook. 'He says, what's your name?' I gave it and the Russian wrote it down. More mumbling. 'He wants to know the name of your family.'

'That is the name of my family.'

More mumbling. 'He wants to know what your own name is.'

'That is my own name, and the name of my family.'

A lot of mumbling and head-shaking. However they seemed to manage to resolve this difficulty.

'He wants to know your rank.'

'Sargurd, yawar, major in English.'

'Ah,' said the Russian officer, 'capataine!'

'No,' I said, 'try one higher', making the appropriate gesture of pointing upwards.

'Ah,' he said again. 'Maiyor.'

'Ji. Han. Yar. Balli,' I said, making various noises of assent. 'Quite right.' He wrote it down. More mumbling.

'He says he wants to see your passport.'

'Tell him I haven't got one,' I replied, being as obtuse as I could.

'He says he is going to the Commandant to tell him that you refuse to show him your passport.'

'Tell him that I haven't got one, but if he wants further proof of what I say he can look at the seals on the official mail bag, and can also see my special pass from the Government of India.'

The officer then examined the seals and labels on the mail bag, taking at least five minutes over it.

'He says he can't read it.'

'Of course he can't. It's written in English.'

'He says, if it had been written in Russian he could read it. Now he says he's gong to tell the Commandant that you won't show him your papers.'

'Tell him I have offered to show him my special pass from the Government of India.'

'He says he would like to see it.'

I got it out and showed it to him. The orderly joined in the long scrutiny.

'He says it ought to be written in Russian because he can't read it.'

'Tell him I am very sorry but the Indian Government does not conduct its business in Russian.'

'He says you ought to have got a translation in Russian from the Russian Legation in Teheran.'

'Tell him that I inquired about this in Teheran, and was told that as I was carrying official mail no special pass was necessary.'

There was then a lot of head-shaking and mumbling.

'He says that he apologises very sincerely for waking you up at this time of night, but that it is his duty and that his duty had to come before all other considerations.'

'That is perfectly all right, and I quite understand.'

'He says he would like to say how sorry he is, but that he had no alternative but to do his duty.'

'Tell him that I quite understand.'

'He says that he did not mean to inconvenience you, but that he had to comply with his orders and that his duty ...'

I began to think that his was growing into a Russian tragedy and that we should all have to weep or drink a bottle of vodka soon, so I put an end to it by holding out my hand and saying good night.

The Russian officer shook my hand and then both he and the orderly saluted smartly. I did my best to reciprocate, but was at a considerable disadvantage in a crumpled pair of not very clean pyjamas which had been doing constant duty for a fortnight, and struggling against continual travelling, dust and dirt. My bare feet did not make me feel any smarter, and my hair was tousled.

Saluting as they went, they withdrew. As they went out through the door, just for the fun of it, I called out after them, 'Good night' in Russian. They turned and looked at me. Eyes talk. Theirs said, 'So the blighter knows Russian after all.'

I returned to bed, and the waiter came back a few minutes later. He said that the Russian officer had said that if he did not come back I would know that the Commandant was satisfied and that everything was all right. I said, 'If they do come back, for heaven's sake give them a bottle of vodka at my expense and make them tight and see them home and tell them to come back at eight o'clock in the morning, by which time I hope I shall have put a trail of dust fifty miles long between myself and this township.'

He continued to tell me the Russians had not come to the pub to see me. They had come to disarm two Persian officers who were in mufti and were carrying revolvers. Then, seeing my car, they had made inquiries about it, and had not believed the waiter when he had told them that it belonged to a British officer who was staying the night in the place.

This next somewhat bizarre encounter took place after the war, in Baghdad in 1948.

On the occasion of another visit to Baghdad, Norman Himsworth, my member of our diplomatic mission there, informed me that he and I had been invited by two senior and influential local officials to dine with them, and spend the evening as their guests.

The place where they chose to entertain us was what? A night club, perhaps. I think not quite that. A restaurant? Something more than that. At all events, the food was very good of its indigenous oriental kind, and there was a continuous cabaret: act after act of multi-toned music; singing – a shade too nasal to be altogether agreeable to occidental ears – accompanied by dexterously fingered stringed instruments and hand- and finger-beaten small drums; and dancing, including of course belly-dancing, but all unexceptionably seemly. ... And our two local hosts were excellent conversationalists and very good company.

There was, too, the fact that the owner of the place and his lively wife, professional middle-class people, perhaps in their mid-thirties, making a hard-earned living out of this local equivalent of inn-keeping, were particularly attentive to us throughout the meal. When we had finished our dinner, they invited us behind the scenes into their own private apartment for coffee, cigars and liqueurs.

We were taken into a quite spacious and comfortable sitting room where two or three of the dancing girls, now changed into normal evening frocks, were relaxing and drinking coffee. We did not sit on the floor. The room was furnished with Western-style soft furnishings, sofas and chairs, with well-chosen Persian carpets underfoot.

There was, however, one extraordinary contrasting feature to the general atmosphere of domestic comfort. On the far end of a divan sat a solitary girl who had not been performing in the cabaret. She was holding a brandy bottle by the neck and, as we came into the room, she waved at us, shouted 'Cheerio!' and took a swig. She then slumped into the divan again. No one seemed to take any notice of her.

We were invited to be seated, and I was placed on the divan next to the brandy girl. As I sat down, she waved the bottle at me, cried out 'Cheerio!', took her swig, and drooped back again into her self-absorbed reverie.

Our hostess having, with her husband, seen to our wants, came and sat on the other side of me and we drank our coffee together. Being naturally interested to know what sort of a life these people had, I managed to get her, and later her husband, to tell me about their business. By hard work, and hard thought, they just about managed to scrape a decent living out of it. It meant late nights always, and a short night's sleep, as they had to be in the market at dawn to get the prime fruit, vegetables, meat and fish that they needed for the restaurant. Having children, it was difficult to make up sleep even at siesta-time in the early afternoon.

Top-class performers for the cabaret were essential to attract a well-heeled clientele who would spend generously. The star of that particular evening, who would be a major draw for the next fortnight, was an Egyptian dancing girl, famed throughout the Middle East. They told me what they had to pay her – somewhat more than the salary of the British Prime Minister. Her beauty was more oriental than occidental – she was a shade too plump perhaps for Western tastes – but, even to my untutored eye, she looked an exceptionally lissom, polished and delicately expressive performer, using every inch of her body, to the very tips of her fingers, to bewitch the audience; and certainly her performance brought the house down, with a chorus of cries of the equivalent of 'encore' for a repetition of her magic. In the relaxed domesticity of our hosts' sitting room, she was modesty itself, quiet and unassertive. It would have been hard to guess that she had the will and determination to put in the long and unremitting hours of practice needed to perfect her act, or that once before the footlights, she could summon up the transcendental magic which had brought her fame.

While engaged in these interesting conversations and reflections, I could not but be constantly reminded of the solitary girl beside me with the bottle of brandy, for the evening was punctuated by her spasmodic cries of 'cheerio!', accompanied each time by another swig. I tried to engage her in conversation, and would have liked to have taken the brandy bottle from her, but she would not speak to me. She seemed entirely self-absorbed.

Then I had an opportunity to ask our hostess about her. What was the matter? Why was she behaving like that? What, indeed, was she doing there?

'Oh, she's one of our dancers; not a star, but one of our own local regular girls. She's a nice girl, and well trained, and she is friendly and the regular patrons like her.' Although not brilliant, and she never would be, her pleasant personality was quite a draw.

'But', I said, 'she wasn't performing tonight.'

'No. We couldn't let her go on tonight; she is in a very emotional state. She has just been jilted by her boyfriend and she's very upset. She's drowning her sorrows, and we think it best to take no notice of her until she feels more composed. The brandy will put her to sleep. She's sound at heart, and she'll be back on the boards in a day or two.'

At that moment there was a crash behind me. 'Cheerio' had fallen off the divan, and the now empty brandy bottle was rolling across the carpet.

Our host and hostess jumped up and went to her, picked her up and carried her out of the room. They were gone some time, we supposed while they were putting her to bed. When they returned, they seemed rather upset, as well they might be at such an occurrence in the presence of honoured guests. So, thanking them for their hospitality, we took our leave and went out into the bright moonlit night, where all was by this time quiet save for the occasional pi-dog baying the moon. And so to bed, having parted from our two distinguished local friends.

Many years later Norman asked me: 'Do you remember the evening at that oriental night club?'

'Yes, very well.'

'Do you recall the "Cheerio" girl?'

'I do indeed.'

'Do you recall that she fell off the end of the divan and had to be carried out?'

'Yes, I do.'

'Do you know what was the matter with her?'

'Yes. She had been jilted, drowned her sorrows in too much brandy, and passed out.'

'No.'

'What then?'

'She was dead.'

Priscilla Napier

A LATE BEGINNER

❧

In her long widowhood Priscilla Napier set up as chronicler of some of her late husband's distinguished forebears – the Napiers of Merchiston spawned a variety of heroes, from the founder of logarithms to the conqueror of Sind. I did five books with her – two on Charles Napier ('I Have Sind: Charles Napier in India 1841–1844' and 'Raven Castle: Charles Napier in India 1844–1851'), then one on his tetchy cousin, Admiral Sir Charles Napier ('Black Charlie'), then a further two on Captain Henry Napier, a less fortunate brother of General Sir Charles. Priscilla wrote with great attack but her narrative pace was leisurely. By the time we got to 'Henry At Sea' and 'Henry Ashore' I thought we must make concessions to an obviously diminishing market. Could she perhaps do some cutting? No, she said, she was only able to make things longer. So we went ahead – tout non court.

'A Late Beginner' is her best book – the 'Times Literary Supplement' reviewer hailed it as 'a triumph' when it first came out (in 1966) and after I had reissued it as one of my Clocktower paperbacks I was gratified to see John Julius Norwich selecting it as his favourite book of memoirs (in a piece for the 'Good Book Guide'). I respect his judgement, and when it overlaps with mine, it's particularly reliable. 'A Late Beginner' is an extraordinarily rich evocation of childhood, full of unexpected turns. Priscilla, born in 1908, spent much of her early life in Cairo, where her father, Sir William Hayter, was legal and sometime financial adviser to the Egyptian government.

A mile or so away, across the other branch of the river, dwelt, had I known it, a sympathiser in the Residency in Cairo, Lord Kitchener.

He had wanted to be Viceroy of India, and they had fobbed him off and made him High Commissioner of Egypt. He made up for his disappointment by proceeding everywhere in the nearest thing that could be managed to vice-regal state. The splendour of his arrival at church was something to stretch the eyes ... My heart, underneath a muslin dress with a wide pink sash, expanded with the glory of it. Possibly Kitchener's did too. Upright, stiff, and gleaming, with his running syces clearing the way before him, he was perhaps able to imagine for a moment that he was Rameses or Alexander, although neither of them can have had those very peculiar *mustachios*. Striding up the church between the canna lilies he seemed stupendous, clinking with medals and giving off a strong dramatic aura of power and vitality. It is improbable that I really remember those eyes close to, focused upon me, that piercing pale blue gaze from irises seemingly too small for their whites. More probably I learnt them later on, from the wartime posters, on which his effigy could be seen, ferociously proclaiming that our King and Country needed us.

Inside, the church, though crammed with people, was cool and quiet, and the roof seemed very high. From outside the roar of Cairo came faintly, the muted ting and rumble of the trams along Boulac, the cries of men with carts ... The parson, the Reverend C. T. Horan, a retired merchant navy captain, gave off an uncomplicated seafaring holiness, conducting the service in an authoritative but gentle manner. Praying, one could feel the pattern of the hassocks imprinting itself interestingly on one's bare knees ...

'Sing the gloria, darling, you know that.' My mother had a veil tied over her large hat; what would happen if she wanted to blow her nose? Behind the lectern, Kitchener, in implacable tones, was reading the Gospel according to St Mark. Over his shoulder one could just see the figure of Christ in a red cloak in the stained glass east window; they looked unlike, but were they relations? How did people stick in hat-pins without sticking them into their heads?

Not all Edwardian men can have had such very long legs: possibly it was one's viewpoint that gave one this impression. Their far up faces, above unaccountably deep collars, seemed always to be breaking into laughter. Their salient characteristic was their relaxedness, a kind of easy-going panache glossing their words and actions. Their legs in narrow trousers carrying them inexhaustibly uphill, or thrown, in gleaming leggings, over a horse's back, moved with an unhurried and purposeful élan. Their voices, heard in mockery, affection, or sternness, rang always with that confident buoyancy that was to sink for ever in the mud of the Great War battlefields, with that unquestioning sense of the rightness and fitness of the Pax Britannica and of their place within it. They basked in what they imagined to be its high noon, in what were in fact its last rays, in the sun never setting upon the regimental band playing selections from 'H.M.S. Pinafore' under the banyan tree. Consciously Christians, of a sort, they fought the good fight against an excess in drinking, smoking or spending; against paying insufficient regard to mothers-in-law or dull old relations. They believed in practically everything, except Father Christmas and votes for women, and it made for great peace of mind ... They believed in right and wrong, with a strong line drawn between. To later critics they could be said to have lived in an innocent, callous, enjoying dream, in some ways perhaps never quite growing up. But they were true to their ethic, and remained, even to people who were not their relations, curiously lovable ... There was something marvellously entire about them.

By the spring of 1913 I could read enough to keep up in the psalms, which made church even more glamorous and exciting. 'My heart is inditing of a good matter,' I shouted, still off key and slightly behind the music, but wildly enjoying it. The roaring indifferent weekday noise of Moslem Cairo outside in the Boulac Road gave one a superb, onward-Christian-soldiers feeling through which the holiness of Mr Horan and his services made a faint occasional dint. Sitting down, if one moved along the pew one could have a cool piece of wood in the pits of one's knees. When that warmed up, one could move back into one's first place where the wood would have cooled. And then back again.

'Don't fidget, darling.'

So much of childhood is frustrating non-communication. One longs to know how to say, 'I am engaged in a purposeful activity that in no way detracts from my participation in the joys of worship.' How lucky that one cannot; or the resolute self-will of infancy would be even more exhausting to cope with than it is.

The Holy Ghost was a character I particularly wanted to get to know better. In the teeth of all the available information, I believed him to be a boy of about fifteen, with wings like a swan and the ability to be in a great many different places at once. Tirelessly on the wing, and with his cheeks for ever bulged out in the manner of the winds in old maps, he blew courage, truthfulness, and a disposition to fold up their underclothes into people's hearts.

On my seventh birthday my mother gave me a Bible and started to read me a chapter every night. We had previously had Hole's 'Illustrated Gospel' every Sunday, accompanied by some gripping Old Testament tales out of a small blue book, but the nightly Bible was promotion indeed. Listening to it I felt momentous, grown-up, and very slightly braver; I began to feel part of what was evidently the winning gang. We read, over the years, clean through the Authorized Version and out the other end. Then we began again.

Nineteen fifteen had a falling away feeling about it. This, sadly, was now revealed to be the last winter of William's company. He was to go to his prep-school in the spring, and be left behind in England when we came back to Egypt in the autumn. No one had consulted me about this arrangement, and I deplored it. Small children seem able to love and resent each other, to miss each other and to be indifferent to each other, all at the same time. I had been grateful to him over baths, in which, owing to my persistent fear of being the baby who went out with the bath-water, he always gallantly took the tap end. I had been jealous of William for being older, for being a boy, for being so much more highly regarded by Mohammed and Abdu and Ahmed and all, for being the centrepiece, for being the right sex in a man's country. He had been jealous of me for my dexterous and deceitful way of getting out of trouble, which he scorned to emulate; for trying to be a pseudo boy and then rapidly switching back into being a little girl when it seemed more politic to trade on the curls and muslin aspect. We had had endless fun. We had enjoyed together those sumptuous and pointless hullabaloos of cheerful din that are so much more satisfactory made by two people than by only one, all those thunderings up and down landings for the sake of thunder, all those shoutings and yellings for the pure joy of noise. We had fought often enough ... Once, in a blood row in the potting shed, I had taken a trowel and scratched his brand new trolley all down its painted side, in revenge for his scorn of my doll's pram, and he had seized up a garden fork and thrown it at me, missing my eye by a fraction of an inch, and leaving a neat little life-long scar on my temple. This was money for old rope. Shining with innocence and streaming with the most satisfactory amount of blood, I had rushed shrieking into the house; making ample capital out of an incident for which I was almost wholly to blame; becoming every instant more tiny, martyred, and female. Perhaps everything in our early life has its point, and sharing a nursery with me steeled William in later years against throwing garden forks at Messrs Bulganin and Kruschev.

(Sir William Hayter became Ambassador in Moscow.)

The zoo at Giza was in a paradisal garden once devised by a millionaire pasha for a much-loved wife. Spacious, and shaded by enormous trees, its paths were mosaiced in bright curlicue patterns of black and red and yellow pebbles. First magnet was the lion house, with its powerful savage smell, and yellow-eyed pacing lions, which one longed to let out, and yet trembled thinking of it. The panther, black as night, lay still, his brilliant eyes stared out past craning heads. Little Egyptian boys gibed at him, threw peanut shells in through the bars of the cages, made sudden loud teasing sounds. There were moments when I hated the Egyptians and this was one. When they tore frogs and nestling birds in pieces at wayside railway stations, in order to induce European passengers to give them money to stop doing it; when, out of nothing but love of exercising pride and power, they incessantly belaboured overladen donkeys who were going the right way anyhow as fast as they could manage; or when, as now, they taunted caged lions, I felt for them a deep belly-loathing, increased by the known futility of intervention. Nor did I reflect that the Egyptians had been more or less so treated themselves, over the centuries, by the Turks and others, and indeed by their own countrymen, and were not in general more cruel than other people. Generally it was difficult not to like them and sympathise with them, so poor, engaging, voluble, and obtuse; haunted by rank misgivings and sustained by garish hopes unlikely of fulfilment.

It is a wonderful thing at eight years old to be in love, when out of sight is truly out of mind. One embraces in an unrecognising manner the idea of love, the feeling of it in the air. In a blissful vacuum of ignorance, one loves without before or after, without suspense, regret or hope. Some new kind of sun has arisen and shines through every unconsciously beguiling aspect of manhood. The loved objects, greatly enhancing life by their presence, are never given a second thought in their absence. They float in a pleasing undifferentiated haze. They could not be contemporaries; for who can love a little boy of eight in khaki shorts and a sun-helmet and front teeth too large for the rest? Probably only his mother: and even so, such soppiness is nigh inconceivable. Otherwise my requirements were simple, and I was in love at Brulos with about ten per cent of the male personnel. They had to be at least as old as fifteen, and under twenty-five, for after that of course decrepitude sets in. I was in love with a young married man called Oliver something, I was in love with the curate, with a wounded soldier on leave, with the man who worked the motor-launch and spoke only Portuguese with a few words of Arabic, with one of the young waiters, with the junior lighthouse keeper, and with a blue-eyed fisherman who cast his net at the mouth of the canal.

Guy Nevill

EXOTIC GROVES
A PORTRAIT OF LADY DOROTHY NEVILL

❧

Lady Dorothy Nevill was born in 1826, a Walpole, daughter of Horatio, 3rd Earl of Orford. 'Like her contemporary, Lady Jeune,' Elizabeth Longford writes in her introduction to Guy Nevill's book, 'she was a Victorian "character" as well as being an exceptional "lady" who went everywhere and knew everyone. One might even call the pair of them the Lady Cunard and Lady Colefax of the nineteenth century. And as Lady Dorothy was compulsively articulate, not to say literary, she became the source of invaluable Victorian and Georgian stories, information and gossip.' Here she is aged ten, travelling across Europe with her father.

The next year [1836], when Dorothy and Rachel were ten and eleven years respectively, the routine of their life was even more interrupted by their father's decision that they should all travel across Europe to Munich. Bad sight was the family malady. Not only had Horatio's sister lost her vision but his son Henry, eight years Dorothy's senior, was blind from birth. So they decided to take him to Dr Walter, the famous German oculist. A party of ten set out including Eliza Redgrave [their governess], two maids, a French cook, and a courier of limited intelligence dressed in gold braid, with two fourgons for the 'batterie de cuisine', six beds which had to be unpacked and made every night, the family coach and barouche, as well as two attendant grooms and six saddle horses, one of which, Testina, seventeen hands and bred for racing, was ridden by ten-year-old Dorothy all the way from Antwerp to Munich. The mare, becoming increasingly temperamental, returned some years later to the racecourse and killed a jockey.

England had been at peace for twenty years, yet the journey through Europe upon which the Orfords embarked was fraught with inconvenience. Horatio's spleen did little to alleviate it. In spite of his previous diplomatic career he had great difficulty curbing his contempt towards foreigners generally, and almost no control over his annoyance with postilions, innkeepers and all officials. But then the English of this period tended to regard foreigners with hostility. During the old wars it was considered policy to indoctrinate the population with a spirit of contempt, which lingered after all reason for it had departed. 'Skip the long words,' said a patriotic tutor to his charges,' they're only the names of foreign countries in which you'll never want to be.'

The existence of so many separate states in Germany caused particularly exasperating delays. Dorothy remembered her father roaring with rage as customs officers effected their boring regulations, while she roasted in the hot sun expecting to faint, pressed by a grumbling crowd. In Italy Horatio outraged the customs officers by screaming in Italian, 'Your king is a swindler.' Apparently not the only one. Hotels or inns were few and far between and fixed tariffs non-existent; mendacious innkeepers believed the English milord was there to be fleeced. They had reckoned without Horatio, however, who was so incensed at the enormous charges levied on candles that he took around an ever-increasing load of partly consumed stumps, until the bag became so heavy it had to be abandoned. The best accommodation they could hope to find was a dusty, uncarpeted room with a brick floor, containing a couple of beds, each big enough to sleep three or four persons, a few wooden, rush-bottomed chairs, a wine-stained deal table, a basin and a jug. The routine became automatic. They would mount the staircase, which had apparently never been washed since the stones were laid, and peruse the bedrooms. Dorothy remembered the horror of beds consisting of boards laid on iron trestles, with a great sack of maize leaves mounted on top, a wool mattress and flat hair cushions as bolster. Admittedly they were generally clean, unlike the staircase, and at least the Orfords and their family never had to survive an ordeal like that of the Duke of Devonshire and his brother who, arriving exhausted at an inn, awoke to discover they were sleeping with a corpse between them.

And here she is, thirty years later, at home at Dangstein, near Petersfield.

Her building became wilder and wilder. A Gothic cottage appeared with intricate dogtooth tiles and slits for shooting arrows, together with aviaries and pigeon lofts, grandly marked 'Dorothy Nevill 1861', a huge tropical palm grotto, and an orchid house (to say nothing of the rain water tank for 11,500 gallons) for which wagon-loads of different sorts of coral toiled up from thc station. As usual the fern house was a major feature, this one being decorated with coral and conch shells set in flint. Dorothy loved it there. She would sit emblazoning and painting china cups and saucers, compiling her snobbish albums, drinking whisky and smoking a cigar, gazing out over her increasingly eccentric demesne. She encouraged visitors, who would be conducted on a grand tour, stopping amid the tropical palms to drink tea which had to be transported a quarter of a mile from the house by panting maids. After this would come the laundry, complete by now with a nice new matron. Not content with ordinary birdsong she had sent off to China for whistles something like small organ pipes made out of gourds, all playing different notes, which she attached to her pigeons' tails – to such good effect that a flight of doves could reasonably be mistaken for a squadron of Aeolian harps.

She was, Guy Nevill points out, a creature of contradictions.

Dorothy in fact disliked being a woman. It stopped her from being accepted in a man's world. She was very annoyed, for instance, not to be able to join Sir Henry Thompson's exclusive male gatherings; he told Dorothy she would have to wear trousers if she came. It was a challenge she often felt like taking up. 'You are your brother in petticoats,' was how Lord Lytton bade goodbye to her after their first meeting, and this was to Dorothy the highest compliment she could be paid.

In 1871 Dorothy had her only daughter, Meresia, presented at court. The social scene had been somewhat penetrated by the daughters of rich Americans who were viewed by Dorothy at first with a certain distaste. On the one hand she wanted to be scientific, tolerant, progressive; on the other she was prejudiced deeply by her previous conditioning. She was deeply suspicious of foreigners and new ways: 'We rather dreaded the social influence of people we did not know,' she observed haughtily, 'and wished the Americans would take away their girls and their tinned lobster.'

She lived to the age of eighty-seven.

Although without firm religious beliefs Dorothy was not frightened by the act of dying. What frightened her was that she might be forgotten like Charlotte Walpole or Lady Cork [her witty crony in Charles Street who had died the previous year]. It was in fact a family trait to wish to make a permanent mark. Some had succeeded; the rest were remembered more for gambling away what the others had accumulated. Would Dorothy only be remembered more for serving up guinea pigs and haunches of donkey? Did she do nothing 'but put food in her mouth and slip gold through her fingers?' It was by now rather late for any fresh assault on posterity. Following Lady Cork's death the family had noticed she was slowing up, although to the public gaze she continued to show the same quaint aspect, appearing at various functions. But soon even in public she began to show symptoms of decay. During Diaghilev's Russian Ballet season at Covent Garden, the author Robert Hichens noticed Dorothy slumped in the stalls, wrapped up in an Indian shawl, asleep.

Michael Russell – 'J. R. Hartley'

FLY FISHING BY J. R. HARTLEY

❧

I've explained in the Introduction the circumstances of my writing the J. R. Hartley books. I've decided to include a few extracts as they're part of the publishing saga; but, as at the time, not everyone will find them an exhilarating experience.

From 'The Holdenhurst Bombardment Cup': General Holdenhurst and J. R. Hartley break off their fishing on the River Wylye to attend the final of the Holdenhurst Bombardment Cup on the local ranges.

'Hoist flags,' General Holdenhurst ordered.

There were two flagpoles adjoining the cup presentation area, on which the flags of the two finalists were now hoisted. The flag of Sheldrake's team was a blue and red affair with an elaborately embroidered cannon with a huge puff of smoke coming out of it, and the legend below 'Steadfast in Bombardment'. The Sharpshooters' flag was dark green with three leeks tied together with a gold bow. Their motto, which particularly caught my attention, was 'Nunc pollicibus venimus demissis'. I turned to the Sharpshooters' adjutant, Captain Williams, and asked him why they'd chosen it.

He looked pleased. 'That's observant of you,' he said. 'There's a story attached to that.'

'Really?' I said.

'Yes,' he went on, 'we advertised for a motto, and a chap from Merthyr Tydfil sent it in. It means "Now we come to the uxorial leeks".'

I considered this for a moment. Then I asked him, 'Which is the word that means "leeks"?'

He made a face. 'Good question. It must be the one beginning with "p". Yes, because "demissis" must be "uxorial", "nunc" is "now" and "venimus" is "we come".'

'No,' I said, 'he was having you on. "Pollicibus" is the ablative of the word for "thumbs".'

'Thumbs?' echoed the adjutant. 'Are you sure it can't sometimes mean "leeks"?'

'Not as far as I know,' I had to tell him. '"Nunc pollicibus venimus demissis" is the processional chorale from a seventeenth-century Crucifixion mass. It means "Here we come with thumbs descending".'

'Blimey,' said the adjutant. 'The colonel'll have a fit. It's a sort of Desert Island Discs thing, is it?'

We were interrupted by an ear-splitting explosion as the first salvo of the final was loosed off just in front of us. I cowered behind Lady Holdenhurst. It seemed to me extraordinary that the general could consider this a spectator sport. After a short while there was a loud cheer as the observers announced 'Direct hit'. Goodbye Devizes.

From 'Putting in the Boot'. Combermere is the Dorset preparatory school where J. R. Hartley works.

Line up all the parents during my time at Combermere and your first choice had to be Mr Ellingham. Admittedly most of them made your selection fairly easy, but Mr Ellingham, without being at all flamboyant, simply looked a success. The headmaster thought he'd bought himself at Harrods. If you had to put your finger on it, Mr Ellingham had finish.

He also had money. He it was who produced a cheque for the entire cost of the new swimming pool before the appeal had even got off the ground; and still waters, as the bursar would keep reminding us with that irritating smirk on his face, cost deep. Those of us who looked upon swimming as more of a threat than a recreation would obviously have preferred to see Mr Ellingham's largesse deployed elsewhere; and as young James Ellingham was one of the boys who came fishing with me, I ventured to joke on his report that we were both looking forward to stocking the new pool with rainbow trout. The rest of the report, both by myself and my colleagues, suggested there was ground to be made up if James was to do himself justice in the coming year's examinations. The unexpected and, as far as I was concerned, fortunate effect of the document on Mr Ellingham was to prompt him to write me a letter wondering if I would consider accompanying them on a fishing holiday in Scotland, giving James 'a little extra tuition between casts'. He apologised that the notice was so short. Yes, I wrote back, I should be absolutely delighted.

He goes to join the Ellinghams and catch the night sleeper to Scotland at Euston Station. Preparing to get on the train …

Distracted, I tripped over a wicker basket containing a child's rabbit which had been standing on the edge of the platform. I was carrying my suitcase in one hand and my rod case in the other, and as I fell, I instinctively thrust out my rod arm, only to lance Lord Justice Grassington in the very moment of his ascending the carriage step. The rod case somehow slipped up the back of his jacket, keeling him over on top of me like an enormous toffee apple, with the result that we were both floundering on all fours when the Ellinghams came running up to help.

James helped me to my feet and recaptured the rabbit, returning it to its owner with the assurance that most rabbits had their ears bent in half like that, which in the relief of being reunited with her pet the child seemed happy to accept. Mr Ellingham, with the perfect balance of levity and concern, was successfully placating Lord Justice Grassington, while Mrs Ellingham stood by exuding the balsam of her blonde good looks.

I felt extraordinarily foolish. If this were symptomatic of my fishing dexterity, what would the Ellingham parents be thinking? As we sat at dinner, with the express in full stride, I had a presentiment that a sudden lurch of the dining car would take me by surprise and I would swoosh my entire plate of veal maréchal all over Mrs Ellingham's canary jumper. I therefore abandoned conventional table manners. I hunched my shoulders to cheat the movement of the train and, in my determination to avoid a second fiasco, lowered my face to within a few inches of my plate.

Mr Ellingham must by now have been having serious misgivings about my inclusion in the party, but he did his best to set me at my ease; and as the threat receded of my deluging Mrs Ellingham with any major percentage of my dinner, I began to recover my confidence. I warmed to these nice people – Mr Ellingham, the socially adroit and polished raconteur, and Mrs Ellingham, always balancing him, quietly assured. I liked the way that now and then she would turn unaffectedly to smile at James; and James would smile diffidently back, with a glance at me to see if I approved these private signals of a happy family life. By the time we swayed off to our respective sleepers and called out our goodnights, I knew that I was going to enjoy myself.

They join the other two married couples, the Charltons and the Turners, at the Station Hotel in Inverness. To explain the subsequent reference to the 'Speakerettes':

Allowing my interest in seventeenth-century history to outmanoeuvre my good manners, I drew attention to the coincidence that Turner and Charlton were successive Parliamentary Speakers in the 1670s. I could tell from their faces, particularly the Speakerettes', that they regarded this announcement as a clumsy attempt to show off my knowledge. There was an awkward silence; I felt myself beginning to go red. Mr Ellingham came swiftly to the rescue, and the faltering conversational engines picked up power again.

The arrival of 'Legs' Maxton later in the holiday is a bad moment.

'It's Legs,' Mrs Charlton suddenly cried, pointing down the glen. A car had crossed the little road bridge over the river and swung left up towards us. It was an enormous Rolls-Royce of unimaginable horse power, one of those special models with a great trunk on the back built just before the war to carry you safely into exile.

Oh, dear, I thought, this a scene from Dornford Yates ...

I waited with a growing sense of disadvantage. When the car slewed to a standstill on the grass in front of us and Legs Maxton got our, my worst fears were realised. He was fine-looking, fortyish, with strong hair and good hands. He had something more than presence, he was an arsenal of personality. When he began to speak he was assured and witty. His voice was resonant and musical. His clothes were perfect. The man was a nightmare ...

They go out fishing after dinner, Maxton keen to impress.

Maxton said he'd take the head of the sea pool, if that suited me, and then fish up to the first bend of the river ... I finally packed up around midnight. Maxton seemed to be having his share of difficulties; I heard cries of frustration further up the bank and occasionally I saw a stab of light from his pencil torch as he must have reeled in for repairs. I left him to it. When I got back to the lodge, Mr Turner was in from the Alder Pool. An empty cointreau bottle was standing on the scales. I turned off the fishing room light and made my way to my room.

The sound of the wicket gate must have wakened me. Having only one bedroom curtain [a cow had put its head through and eaten the other] I was able to pull myself up and peer out of the window without getting out of bed. Those who have fished at night in the north of Scotland at that time of year will know that there is a surprisingly short time of total darkness, and certainly I had no difficulty in making out the figure of Legs Maxton going to the boot of his Rolls-Royce and removing from it three packages. I watched him unwrap them. Each contained a very handsome fish.

It was not long before I heard him going upstairs to bed. I gave him about twenty minutes, then I got up, eased open my bedroom door and tiptoed to the fishing room. There on the table, beside my finnock, were Maxton's gleaming impostors. The dishonour of the man astounded me. I gathered up the fish, went out to the Rolls-Royce and replaced them in the boot. The house was sleeping. I returned to bed and lay there in a state of exultation.

Breakfast at Inverpolly Lodge was at nine. Thanks to Mrs Grantley's lavish interpretation of our requirements it was fully and punctually attended. On this particular morning nothing would have made me late. I sat down at the table a few minutes early with a cup of coffee and my book.

Maxton came down last and I waited for him to go over to the serving table. I began by asking Mr Turner whether there'd been any action at the Alder Pool. He gave me a thumbs down sign across the table. I could see Maxton waiting for my question with a practised nonchalance. I asked him how he'd got on.

'Beginner's luck,' he replied. 'I had three rather nice ones.'

'Three?' I enthused. The Speakerettes were all but toppling off their chairs. 'Where did you catch them?'

'One just by the plank bridge, the other two up by the reeds on the far side.'

'Gosh,' I said, 'that's smart casting.'

He returned to the table with his breakfast, rationing his smile.

It was all too much for the Speakerettes. 'Come on everyone,' called out Mrs Turner, 'let's see Legs's fish.'

I let them go ahead of me. When I followed them into the fishing room there was already a great flutter.

'Is there a cat or something?' Maxton was asking.

'Perhaps they weren't quite dead,' Mrs Turner suggested, 'and they started to flip flop back where they came from.'

'It's a strong instinct with fish,' I said, 'but they can't always open the door.'

When I looked at Maxton he seemed a genuinely puzzled man. When, later in the day, I happened to see him walking back from his car, he was like a man to whom light has been revealed when darkness is the kinder option. I think I must have smiled because he looked at me with an expression that passed from realisation into something very close to hatred.

Good old Headquarters.

From 'Marriage Lines', in which Hartley and his wife go fishing in Skye.

It was in the south of the island, at Loch Coruisk, that we ran into Hamish, perhaps the most lugubrious man the world has ever seen. He was waiting when we arrived and nodded a greeting without actually delving into his vocabulary. He was dressed cautiously for a brightish summer day, with defences of tweed and waterproof that would have been more suitable for an afternoon out with Grace Darling. He worked his lips backwards and forwards over his dentures, pulled on a sou'wester, and gazed round at the weather, which to our untutored eyes looked almost flawless. 'Dour,' he said after a while, 'verra dour.'

Hamish infuriates them and they deliberately leave his haversack behind.

At the end of the day he started up the outboard and we chugged out through the gap of the loch, out of the clutch of the Cuillins and into the sea. Soay, Rhum and Canna lazed in the evening light ahead of us. The wind had dropped, all Hamish's dire predictions were confounded. And he had worse to come. Helen and I, together in the bow, sat huddled in the warmth of our little conspiracy, watching the blue peaks receding behind us and the turning tide clawing at the shore. Then, with the boat's white wake tracking round in a widening arc over the swell, we came into view of the lodge at Camasunary, held in the flat palm of the hinterland between the hills. And we laughed at Hamish's disapproving figure hunched over the tiller at the other end of the boat, and at our pleasure in each other, the time ahead of us, and the spell of the sea and the sky.

The engine died away and we felt the scrunch of the boat grounding, freed for a moment as Hamish climbed out into the water to draw us in. Helen pulled out the bundled picnic rug and stood there with it in her arms waiting to get out. Then, with Hamish standing malignantly by the boat's mooring post, we prepared to make our farewells.

'Where's ma sack?' he asked eventually.

Helen affected dismay. 'It's by a rock at our picnic place,' she said. 'Oh, don't say you want it.'

The gloom in Hamish's voice had a musical quality. He forced out the words. Of course he wanted it.

'You should have said,' Helen told him.

We set off along the steep pony path, five hundred feet up and then on to where we'd left the car. We turned at the top to look back at that stunning view over Camasunary to the Cuillins. Just emerging from Loch Coruisk we saw Hamish in the cockle of discontent, the haversack presumably retrieved.

We watched together for a while with vindictive satisfaction. Then we walked on to the car, in the earnest hope it wouldn't let us down. It started first time and we bumped away round the top of Loch Slapin to Broadford and our friends.

J. R. HARTLEY CASTS AGAIN

Trouble at the school pantomime. J. R. Hartley has been persuaded by the bursar, the pantomime's producer, to do the audience participation number as 'Giant Waders' with an embarrassing number called 'Watch Out, Mr Trout'.

It was in the Glade in the Forest on the Way to Transylvania that things started to go wrong. I was by now in an agony of apprehension, balanced on my half-stilts, fingering my rod and beset by the imminence of the audience participation number. The bursar, irritatingly cocky, was standing in the wings in front of me accompanying the modulations of his script with wavy gestures. I saw Miss Craigie look round the huge oak glade, sigh and declare that it reminded her of her beloved Scotland ...

The chances of Miss Craigie fluffing the lyrics of 'Loch Lomond' were nil, so it was a reasonable moment for the prompter to take time off to hold the ladder while the carpenter hoisted into place the billboard containing the lyrics of 'Watch Out, Mr Trout', which was the next feature scheduled for the Glade. So as Miss Craigie, in a Force 8 contralto, debated the alternative routes to the Highlands, Mrs Macdonald-Macdonald left the prompter's chair, to which her dog Fortinbras was securely tied, and went to Mr Judd's assistance.

Fortinbras was a smooth-coated dog with a very pointed face that was ideal for examining other animals' parts. It was a nice dog, but a dog whose curiosity could sometimes get the better of its obedience. As it watched Miss Craigie singing her kilt off in the Glade, it became aware that in the temporary absence of its mistress a closer look, a guest appearance even, was an available option. So it ventured out on to the boards, towing the chair behind it.

This was a great success with the more frivolous elements of the audience, less so with the animal's co-proprietor, Major Macdonald-Macdonald, who was seated in the front row alongside the headmaster. A breakdown in pet discipline was not the Major's cup of tea.

He stood up.

'Myrna,' he shouted, 'Fortinbras is on the stage.'

Mr Westacott, put off by this interruption no more than a yard or two away, faltered at the Upright Oldham [a little-known make of piano that looked like a boarding-house washstand]. Mr Pringle's trumpet died to a brass yawn. Miss Advani, revolving to keep her options open, kept up a sort of caretaker pizzicato on the 'cello.

'Fortinbras,' the Major bellowed, giving each syllable equal and extended emphasis, 'get off, you pointed sod.'

This was unexpected competition for Miss Craigie's rendering of 'Loch Lomond'. It also produced an unfortunate chain reaction. Myrna Macdonald-Macdonald abandoned her supervision of the ladder, which fell sideways against the back of the flat, which in turn fell forwards on to the stage, revealing a number of the production staff in informal pose. The carpenter lost control of the lyric board of 'Watch Out, Mr Trout', which crashed down within inches of Miss Craigie, then toppled forward into the orchestra pit, dispersing the trio and causing some superficial damage to the Upright Oldham. It was followed almost immediately, like a windfall apple, by the carpenter. Fortinbras, startled, struck off backstage, still towing his chair.

Miss Craigie, like the good trouper she was, stood by the dictum that the show must go on. She hitched up her kilt and broke into her number again. Mr Pringle and Miss Advani soon caught up with her, although Mr Westacott was deflected by urgent repairs to the Upright Oldham.

I looked to see the effect of all this on the bursar. He was stooping forward, pressing the top of his head, as if to force it down his neckshaft into the concealment of his chest. The word 'rout' was written all over the production. I think I went mad. Miss Craigie deserved some moral support. I decided to take a hand.

Striding on in my half-stilts, clutching my rod, I entered what was left of the Glade. There was a surge of applause. Miss Craigie, singing of the bonny banks, smilingly nodded acknowledgement of my show of solidarity. Bringing my line back through the gap in the scenery, I sizzled it out over the audience. Major Macdonald-Macdonald was still upright in the front row, shouting to his wife to re-establish control of Fortinbras, and I think in recovering my line I may just have clipped the back of his head. It may have been this that got the better of his self-control, or it may have been his wife's ham-fistedness in detaching Fortinbras from the chair and then accidentally letting go of him so that he reappeared on stage and started barking at Miss Craigie. Most likely it was a combination of the two, though from what I knew of the Major's makeup, the double public disgrace of indiscipline from his dog and incompetence from his wife would have weighed the heavier. He charged the stage.

This was a bemedalled veteran of the Western Front, a man you wouldn't stop without several rolls of barbed wire and a company of sharpshooters. In fact he was after Fortinbras, but Mr Westcott thought he was after me and tried to block him with the Upright Oldham. The Major brushed it aside like a matchbox, and scrambled up the parapet that separated the orchestra from the stage. Something told me, with clear enunciation, that the time had come to make for the wings. I threw down my rod and went as fast as my stilts would carry me. I heard the bursar calling 'Curtain, curtain', but the carpenter, whose responsibility this was, still lay immobilised on stage.

All seemed lost. But then occurred a series of miracles. The brief intervention by Mr Westcott had added crucial seconds on to the Major's charge, with the result that when he got on to the stage not only had I left it but his wife had appeared helter-skelter, snatched up Fortinbras, and rushed off again with the dog under her arm. Even the carpenter was beginning to crawl slowly towards the wings. So the Major, with audience interest behind him at fever pitch, found himself face to face with Miss Craigie with no mission left to perform. To our amazement he began to join Miss Craigie in a duet, singing in a very decent and unselfconscious baritone. Miss Craigie, beaming, opened up like a giant Venus flytrap and captivated the audience's affections in one swallow. Together the soloists came front stage, their arms extended forward in a trident, as if to spear the participation of the house. [The Major had lost an arm in the service of his country.] They succeeded. At first rather wavering and apologetic, the singing gathered authority, then swelled out of all proportion, backed by a rhythmic clapping of hands. From the safety of the wings I couldn't believe it; and this was but the start of Providence's intervention.

Hartley is invited over with a pathetic pupil to the boy's affluent grandparents' house (from 'A Matter of Honour').

'Do you play football?' Captain Striding asked. 'Because you're going to have to.'

The words hit me. I couldn't get out of the way.

'I haven't played for years,' I said. 'Fishing's more my thing.'

'Well, we'll go on the river tomorrow morning. But I've said you'd keep goal for the village against Cridland's Biscuits. They're a Warminster outfit.'

'What's happened to the regular goalkeeper?' I asked.

'Bust his arm.'

'He'd still be better with one arm than I would with two.'

The Captain looked at me a little reprovingly.

'Come on,' he said, 'Michael billed you as the great Combermere sportsman.'

I knew I shouldn't have come.

'I haven't any football clothes,' I said desperately.

'You can borrow my boots,' the Captain said. 'They scored two goals against Cambridge.'

'Yes,' I said, 'but they probably had your feet in them. I'm useless. Your team will be disqualified from the league.'

'Not from the Coriolanus League, Division Four,' the Captain replied confidently.

'Couldn't you play?' I asked.

He shook his head. 'I'm the non-playing captain.'

'Well,' I said, hoping I detected a chink, 'couldn't you be the playing non-captain? Just for once?'

'Wouldn't do. I just lend them the pitch.'

We sat down to lunch. Sobs [Michael] was watching our conversation from the other side of the table like a spectator at a tennis match.

The Captain's talk crackled with sporting allusions. When I asked him about the respective merits of Winchester and Salisbury Cathedrals, he said that at Salisbury it was probably all of an 8 iron from the west door to the chancel steps. You won't find that in Pevsner.

'I hope the defence is reliable,' I said when he had evidently exhausted his companion guide to the Cathedrals.

'The left and right back are mustard,' the Captain reassured me with a mouth full of lettuce. 'They work on the farm here. They're twins. The Andrews brothers.'

Well, at least it was the brothers.

Hartley is asked by a pupil's parents to go fishing in Scotland in the holidays (from 'The Enemy').

The Frenches would already have gone up to Scotland by the end of the summer term, so their son Rupert was to travel up with me on the night sleeper. I was invited to spend a week with them in the lodge they had taken near Fort William for fishing on the River Lochy. It was the usual arrangement, light instruction for the boy, whom I'd already been teaching on the Axe, and making up the party. Helen was happy for me to go on my own; she said it was work. By which she meant the Frenches and their friends.

Rupert was coming into his last year at Combermere, so I knew the parents a little. Giles French was a billbroker, which involved, as far as I could understand, walking round the City in a silk hat between the hours of ten and three and taking a modest turn on several million times my life's earnings several times a day, depending presumably on how fast he walked. It didn't sound very interesting but it sounded a fairly reliable way of funding fishing holidays. Mrs French was pleasant and smartly decked out, the boy was nice enough too – neither very bright nor very dim, with strong honey-coloured hair that had had a lot of brushing in the years before he got to Combermere, and plain honest looks. If the school outfitters had stocked boys to match the clothes list, it could well have been Rupert French they took down from the shelves.

Going north to fish always put me in a good mood; any inconveniences in the journey receded in the pleasures of arrival – the spice of anticipation in the early morning air and the evocative station sounds. Rupert was excited and blooming with liberation: I remembered from the start of my own school holidays that feeling of almost sensual adjustment, the feeling of being suddenly out of range. We had dinner in the dining car. He waited to hear what I was ordering and said that was just what he'd like too. We talked easily, the two of us together still in the relationship of school; but when his mother came to collect us in the morning I could tell that my holiday status – of something between guest and hireling – upset our more formal but easier conventions.

Mrs French was very welcoming without quite being warm. The same applied to Fort William, where we paused to shop: there was a slightly Calvinistic, Sunday-suited feel about the slate-roofed buildings, some dark grey stone, some rendered and whitewashed, rising steeply from the narrow pavements. We called in at the Rod and Gun Shop, half way down the main street, and I bought some flies and spare tackle. They managed the Town Water and several other Lochy beats in there and they could give me cautionary words that I'd be 'nae wise' to neglect some extra one or other of their wares. The salmon seemed to like their patterns not too bright. If so, they did well to home in on Fort William.

Hartley is fishing on the River Teifi in Wales with his old friend Henry Fisk (from 'The Tip Off').

We fished quite late, with no results. The evening was fine and serenely beautiful, strapping down the landscape in swathes of dark shadow. There was a feeling of closing time on the river, with just a hint of mist. We packed up by the car and compared notes on the day. I shouldn't have liked to count the number of evenings I'd stood like that with Henry, ever since those first undergraduate days on the Coln, being driven down from Oxford in our tutor's car, with war in the offing and all our impressions daubed in the strong colours of youth. Now we had the confidence of tested friendship to indulge each other's enthusiasms, to be fishing bores without boring each other; and our wives sensibly left us to it.

To Ireland with Uncle Reggie (from 'About Tern').

Neither Lawrence, Helen nor I had been to Lough Corrib before. Uncle Reggie claimed to have fished there 'once or twice', but when we were trying to establish which was the best place to stay, I had to read out several place names from the map. Uncle Reggie was sure it began with a 'C', on the south-western shore of the lough. Then he agreed it might be Oughterard. He wrote off to book rooms.

We flew to Dublin in a Viscount. I am nervous about air travel and I consider even four engines an inadequate hedge against the dangers. But this was rather like flying breast stroke, not exhilarating but not unduly alarming, though it helped to see the Rolls-Royce symbols on the engines as the tiny ridges of the Irish Sea edged slowly under the outline of the wings.

I love going to Ireland but I don't think I could live there. I suffer from a sense of order; when things get difficult I need there to be a shoulder to the wheel. In England we've got used to a shortage of shoulders, but in Ireland there probably isn't a wheel.

We were to stay overnight at the Shelburne Hotel. 'Start as you mean to go on,' Uncle Reggie kept saying expansively at lunch, clicking his fingers for the waiters. Afterwards he set out for the shops and was away about an hour before returning with twelve silk shirts from Tyson's, a quantity of slightly unnecessary fishing tackle and a stuffed Caspian tern in a glass case. I have no idea what sort of price he paid for the bird nor what sort of shopkeeper has the optimism to hold that sort of stock; but Uncle Reggie was delighted and made me accompany him to the public library to find out from the 'Handbook of British Birds' a little more about the species. This necessitated taking the creature with us and there was some doubt at the door whether the rules of the library were being breached by allowing it admittance. But we explained that it was too static to constitute a pet and we needed to bring it in to check its appearance against the reference books. The staff saw the validity of this and one of them kindly helped us in our researches, agreeing with us that its size and handsome red bill made it a Caspian tern beyond dispute.

Uncle Reggie was cockahoop, as we set off back to the hotel, that the 'Handbook' conceded less than forty United Kingdom sightings. 'It's the bargain of the century,' he said. 'I bet that shopkeeper thought it was a seagull.'

At risk of being a wet blanket I had to point out that, though a live United Kingdom sighting would be an ornithological bullseye, a dead specimen might have come from anywhere. The Caspian tern is an almost cosmopolitan species. Uncle Reggie fell silent at this and it was only when we were approaching the Shelburne, along St Stephen's Green, that he popped up in his historical nugget mood with a little sweetmeat about the Dutch East India Company's early attitude to buggery at sea.

'Both of them over the side,' he said. 'No messing about.'

'Well, no more messing about,' I agreed.

'Bit rough though, isn't it?'

Yes, I said, it didn't seem very broad-minded.

GOLFING BY J. R. HARTLEY

This came out in 1995. It was an effort to squeeze a few more drips out of the lemon, and indeed a few drips duly appeared. Yellow Pages had been running a television advertisement in which our hero had taken up golf, so the brief was to concoct nine self-contained golfing stories with wide-ranging locations. (For the Irish one, Lahinch was indulgently allowed to accommodate my 'Anyone for Ennis?') For accuracy I had to check up on the individual courses – I think the secretary of the Ilkley Golf Club must have been rather puzzled to be asked on the telephone which of the holes there ran alongside the River Wharfe.

The one that follows is abridged from 'The Caddie'. If you're still there, you'll see what I mean.

Tiger McCabe is J. R.'s golfing friend, a victim of Army cutbacks. 'It seems a betrayal when an institution that's so good at making you feel important suddenly informs you that you're not. Tiger hadn't got all that far, but he was on the escalator of commissioned rank and if there are two things that characterise an escalator, one is continuity and the other – assuming you've got on the right side – ascent. The last thing you expect is that it should stop. Tiger's had.'

He had arranged a game for us at one of the smart courses near London. We were booked in with a member, one of Tiger's old comrades-in-arms. He was an eight handicap player and took his game seriously. Tiger hoped I wouldn't find him too much of a stickler. 'Give me a stickler any day of the week,' I said. 'You know where you are with a stickler.' Admittedly it isn't always where you want to be, but I didn't want to prejudice the outing.

Tiger also mentioned that he was bald with conspicuously big eyebrows. He was sensitive about that; for some reason people found it funny. I said it didn't sound that funny to me. It sounded like a slight distribution problem, but that wasn't something you laughed at.

Tiger looked at me suspiciously. 'Bald and bus jokes are absolutely out,' he said. 'Anything about two more on top and you're dead meat.'

I thanked him for the warning. It struck me that the Colonel must be a formidable customer if Tiger, who wasn't exactly timid, thought he needed handling instructions. I didn't like the sound of him.

'And I beg of you not to be late,' Tiger said. 'We're due to meet at the clubhouse at ten past nine on the whistle.'

'I'll be there,' I said.

Then I found I'd muddled up my dates and I'd be staying a good three hours' drive away. I didn't mention it to Tiger; the arrangements were all made and he was jumpy enough already that something might go wrong. There seemed no alternative but to drive down for the game and drive back afterwards; and keep quiet that I'd done it.

I apologised to my host and hostess in advance. They knew that golf was my new enthusiasm, but wasn't driving that far taking one's pleasures a little over-seriously? I explained that it was really down to Colonel Buss. If you made a plan with Colonel Buss you were expected to cross hemispheres to keep it. My host said he certainly wouldn't; you simply didn't make plans with people like that.

However I had; or worse, Tiger had for me. They probably still thought I'd cancel once I got up there, but my mind was made up.

My hostess offered to get me early breakfast before I set off. No, I said, absolutely not, nobody was to move; I'd slip out as quiet as a mouse, or, as it turned out, as quiet as a mouse that knocks a montage of Ashanti spears off the stairs wall …

I drove up to the clubhouse at seven minutes past nine. Tiger was already there, talking to someone who was obviously Colonel Buss and another man I assumed to be Dr McGarry. The Colonel had mentioned that Dr McGarry would be the fourth. We gathered that he was eleven handicap and had invented some sort of electronic valve that enabled him to retire from inventing and spend a lot of time on the golf course.

I took to him at once. He spoke very quietly, with a face full of amusement. He was unassuming, benign and unusual, a sort of human four leaf clover. He was probably also very clever, but he didn't wear his cleverness like a threat; whereas Colonel Buss was vigorously assertive, physical and galvanising, a sort of human starting handle. Just when he stood in front of me, I felt he was bombarding me with ions.

I had some small talk with Colonel Buss. Very small talk. I was careful not to look too hard at his eyebrows in case he thought I was making implicit comparisons with his bald head. As a result I must have seemed a little shifty. Tiger kept intervening on my behalf, like a mother for a small child.

'Is it the first time you've played here?' Colonel Buss asked.

'Yes, I think you said it was, didn't you?' Tiger said before I could come out with a simple yes myself.

'You'll enjoy it,' predicted Colonel Buss. 'It separates the sheep from the goats.'

That didn't sound much of a plus. I don't know which of those two creatures is worse at golf, but that's the group in which Colonel Buss obviously included me …

The Colonel had hired caddies for everybody, 'his treat' he said, although it didn't look much of a treat to me. Mine was a veteran called Jack. He had rather a cross face as if he'd always been looking into bad weather, but he was perfectly agreeable …

Jack offered to get my clubs out of the car. I gave him the keys and he said he'd see me on the first tee. Colonel Buss shepherded us along, then started doing some loosening up exercises. He seemed very disciplined. First he did some swings with his left arm only, and finally some sizzling full practice swings. He looked a class performer. His drive howled off the tee.

Tiger drove for our side, long but slightly off line. The four of us, with the four caddies in two pairs just behind us, strode off up the fairway. The sheep were about to be separated from the goats. I began to feel a little nervous.

I should have felt much more nervous had I known that my bag was full of drain covers. On my way to where I was staying I had called in on my daughter in the Midlands. My clubs were in the boot of my car and, while I was indoors having tea, my grandson and a small friend had filled the bottom of the bag and the pockets with all the drain covers that served the downpipes round my daughter's house and two of her neighbours' houses as well. They were of that design that gets clogged with leaves in the autumn which you prod out with a pencil. I'd noticed the two boys were giggling when they said goodbye but hoped the joke was at the expense of my daughter rather than myself. Which to some extent it was, though not enough.

The game progresses. Jack the caddie

seemed to be toiling; I had the impression that all wasn't quite well. He looked at me once or twice a little quizzically, but said nothing about the weight of the bag. At the seventh his stride began to shorten and Tiger asked me on the quiet whether there was someone in my bag. I'm afraid I laughed it off. I said that if you carried golf bags as a profession, in the course of a career you'd expect to shoulder the odd stowaway. I somehow didn't like to ask Jack if there was anything wrong. It never occurred to me that it could be the weight, and he'd surely say if he wasn't feeling well. So I said nothing, although he was puffing out his cheeks and generally looking very short of oil.

Just before the turn, halfway up a short steep incline, he made an odd neighing noise and subsided suddenly onto the ground. Our opponents and their caddies were up ahead; Tiger and I ran to his aid.

'That's a heavy bag,' he said, in the voice that actors in Westerns tend to use when they've just stopped three bullets in the chest in the town saloon. It's slow and pensive and usually heralds expiry, although Jack didn't look that far gone.

'Take it easy,' I said, loosening his collar, 'take it easy.' Then I lifted the bag away from him. He had a point when he said it was heavy. I stared at it in disbelief.

Tiger's caddie slipped away to signal to the others that we had a problem. I say we, but Jack in particular. They came back to join us, just in time to see a series of drain covers come clattering out of my bag as Tiger upended it on the fairway.

Colonel Buss looked from the drain covers to the seized up caddie and back again. Rational conclusions seemed to elude him. 'For Heaven's sake,' he said.

I was seriously rattled. I felt that I was in a crisis that was determined to become a disaster, something which was going to happen simply because it would be so appalling if it did. Jack was going to be permanently struck down and Colonel Buss and the rest of them would think it was my fault; there'd be resentful relatives and crippling litigation. I could tell from the look on Colonel Buss's face that it didn't occur to him that I was the victim of a trick. I don't know if he thought I was making off with the church roof, but I could see he was having doubts about my suitability to be included in a foursome in his company and on his course. And that was nothing to what he was going to think if the pile of drain covers was topped up in the next few minutes by a dead caddie.

I looked at Jack. He was very red in the face but he didn't look to be in pain. One of the caddies knelt beside him, half propping him up while he lay back with his eyes closed, breathing heavily. 'Please live,' I begged him silently.

'What shall we do with him?' Colonel Buss muttered to the rest of us.

We could all see the man was being inconvenient and there was a foursome coming up behind, but I thought a little more warmth of spirit mightn't have been out of place. Dr McGarry evidently thought the same.

'Give him a minute,' the caddie who was propping him up said, 'and he'll be just fine.'

That was what I wanted to hear. There was a reassuring note of experience, too, a hint of I've seen this before, although I can't believe there was a precedent in the profession for anyone being floored by drain covers. Perhaps he was just sticking up for the side.

We'd been asked to give him a minute. It passed. Colonel Buss was getting visibly fussed about the foursome behind. He turned to Dr McGarry.

'Do you think we should let them through?' he asked.

'Yes,' said Dr McGarry, 'but I'm rather more concerned about Jack.'

Colonel Buss said something about the man being all right in another minute or two, then waved the foursome through. He looked with concern at the drain covers lying on the fairway.

'Get that junk out of the way,' he said to his caddie, 'they'll wonder what the hell we're playing at.'

As his colleague started to gather up the drain covers, the patient suddenly sat up, shook his head, apologised and pronounced himself recovered. Colonel Buss looked at us all with a told-you-so expression and deputed Dr McGarry's caddie to accompany Jack back to the clubhouse. At this Jack protested unconvincingly that he was all right to go on.

'You're not,' the Colonel said sharply. 'You've given us all a nasty shock.'

Jack looked shamefaced and apologised a second time, attributing his indisposition to too much digging in his allotment. Then he allowed himself to be escorted away.

The other caddie had by now moved the drain covers off the fairway and was looking enquiringly at Colonel Buss as to what he should do with them. The Colonel clearly wanted them dumped, but I wasn't having that. They had work to do back in the Midlands. So before the Colonel could give instructions I told the caddie that I'd take charge of them. I took off my pullover, loaded the pile into it, knotted the arms together, and announced I'd carry the drain covers if someone else could take my bag. The look on the Colonel's face suggested that he considered he was being unnecessarily exposed to public ridicule and that he wished there were someone present who could twiddle a ring and make him disappear. Tiger said he'd carry his own bag, and his caddy could take mine.

I heaved the drain covers along for the rest of the round. They had an awkward habit of bouncing up and down in my pullover, and the weight of them stretched the sleeves. But, though I've seen stranger things in books of home remedies, I'd never have expected to find myself recommending a jerseyful of drain covers if you want to clip a few shots off your golf score. I played like a demon. Dr McGarry dubbed me 'the magic plumber'. Colonel Buss exuded dislike. We won two and one.

Jack was sitting on a bench in front of the clubhouse, waiting to signal himself all right on our return. I bought him a bottle of whisky and made the mistake of asking him about his allotment. He ran through a dispiriting litany of vegetable lore, which I had eventually to interrupt, with a smiling apology, and make my way to where Colonel Buss was waiting to say goodbye. I knew my stock, already low, had sunk to nothing. He shook hands with passable grace, thanked me for the game, then added witheringly, 'Good luck with the drains.'

'Thank you,' I said. 'And good luck with the hair.'

I rang my host and hostess to say I was coming up via my daughter's. 'We'll see you when we see you,' my hostess said, with more than a grain of truth.

The drain covers are returned to their owners. The culprits are nowhere to be seen.

When I got in, my host and hostess had just finished rearranging the montage of Ashanti spears, which I'd left in a pile on a hall chair with a note of apology on the top. The mishap seemed nicely to symbolise our colonial collapse, although my host and hostess may have seen it simply as an act of clumsiness.

'A long day,' my host said. 'How did it go?'

I decided only on the broader picture. 'We won two and one,' I said.

Priscilla Scott-Ellis

THE CHANCES OF DEATH
A DIARY OF THE SPANISH CIVIL WAR

edited by Raymond Carr

❧

Priscilla ('Pip') Scott-Ellis, a daughter of the 8th Lord Howard de Walden, went to the Spanish Civil War as a nurse on the Nationalist side – her allegiance not so much a matter of considered political assessment as because her family were friends of the Spanish royal family. Her diary ran to over half a million words – it was a major bonus that so eminent an authority as Raymond Carr agreed to edit it. He writes in his Introduction:

Pip had no strong convictions either political or religious. To keep up appearances she attended Mass with her friends, all of whom shared the belief in the war as a crusade against the atheists, masons and Communists of the Republic. Her political convictions were naïve in the extreme and she swallowed uncritically the Francoist propaganda and shared the monarchist convictions of her friends: the Republicans were 'Reds' and barbarians who used dum dum bullets and burnt churches ...

Apart from its interest as a human document revealing the secret life of a truly extraordinary woman and as a historical document that gives both a picture of life in the Nationalist zone and a vivid, and at times terrifying, description of the state of the Nationalist hospital services, the fascination of the diary lies in the contrast between the dirt and squalor of life in the hospitals in which she served, and what she calls the 'other life' that centred round the Infantes and their children and their aristocratic friends.

When she arrived in Spain the war had been going on for just over a year. After training as a nurse in Jerez, she was sent to an 'equipo' (clearing station) in Aragon. Here she is dealing with casualties from the Battle of Teruel – it was estimated that the Nationalists suffered 16,000 wounded in their successful attack.

Saturday, 19 February [1938]. A hard day's work at the hospital. We never stopped all day. Ten operations: 6 stomach wounds, 3 heads, one arm amputated and one man who was wounded in the lungs who died on the stretcher before they could operate him. We had just got back from a hasty lunch of fried potatoes and foul tinned meat and found him on the stretcher obviously dying. Consuelo sent for the priest to give him the Last Sacrament and we could do nothing at all, just sat around miserably watching him die. He was unconscious and as pale as a sheet. We looked through his pockets to see if there was any address of his family to write to, but only found one pathetic crumpled letter from his fiancée saying that, after all the difficulties there had been with her family, when he came back from the war they would let him marry and how happy they would be. It was pathetic reading it with him dying at our feet. As there was no address we can't even write to tell her what has happened to him. The worst was that there was a hurry to start operating another, the 'capitan', who is a brute, got angry and told them to take him away to the mortuary for the dead and the man was still living. Suppose he came to life to find himself just thrown anyhow amongst the dead corpses or buried alive. It must happen to lots of them. I have seen them being taken away to the cemetery just piled up anyhow half-naked in a lorry. It is foul and not necessary. All morning aeroplanes were roaring overhead but I had no time to watch them. Twenty-one Red machines came over but we did not know it all till after as they did not bomb us. I don't know where they went to. A head of Sanidad turned up to make a registration of all the 'equipos' and told us that now there are only to be ten movable 'equipos' and we are one of them, which means that we will always be sent to wherever the war is hardest, which is exactly what we want.

'Pip [writes Raymond Carr] was particularly fond of the Infanta Beatrice (Princess Bee in her diary) and of her son Ataulfo. Ataulfo was a navigator attached to the Condor Legion, the German unit serving with the Nationalist forces.'

Saturday, 19 March [1938]. I woke at eight feeling tired but a new woman. More casualties had just come in, after leaving us a peaceful night, thank God, so went to find the ward in the most appalling mess with pools of blood everywhere, all the beds dirty and unmade. I went to our small ward to fetch more sheets and found five dead corpses strewn anyhow on the floor, which made a pleasant aperitif to breakfast. We worked all morning straightening things out, giving injections etc. A few new patients came in and one or two were operated, but too much happens here for me to remember it all. By midday we had everything tidy so went to sit on the patio in the sun making numbers of the beds and lists of things, when Ataulfo appeared. He was very worried about us having been in Escatrón during the bombardments. He was quite right to be worried as he came through there today and says there is scarcely anything left of it, and he would not have recognized it as the same town. He says that Princess Bee disapproves of my leading this life and thinks it is time I went away. I said she was quite wrong, and we argued a lot about it. He threatened to send the Infanta to fetch me, but I begged him not to. I do hope he won't as I can't say no to her, and yet I have no intention of leaving. Maybe if he had asked me to leave yesterday evening I would have done so with joy, but last night I slept and now things are very different. He brought us biscuits, chocolate, shortbread and wine, but alas no cigarettes and he has run out too. He has promised to see what he can do about my stolen car, as of course it has not turned up. At about six three or four wounded arrived. Two were operated, which meant everything was just nicely finished off for dinner. All through dinner we were saying how gorgeous to go to bed in peace when suddenly a head casualty arrived, followed quickly by a stomach, two legs, a hand and an arm. As they all arrived at once and we have only a limited quantity of oil lamps it was complete chaos. The floor was covered in stretchers, blood everywhere, everyone shouting, the poor patients moaning and screaming, and so instead of going to bed it started all over again. One thing is that though there is a certain amount of bombarding here and lots of shells fall in the town, so far none have fallen very near us. One or two did yesterday and a few this afternoon, but nothing to worry about. Three patients had to be operated, one stomach, one hand amputation and one arm. At 3 o'clock I went to bed as everything had settled down again. Consuelo stayed to cope till it was all finished. She had a bad time with a head who died screaming and fighting and cursing. Most heads seem to go mad, they are the ones I loathe as they have a glassy look in their eyes and make awful noises and are quite crazy. I don't really see how we can go on like this, working all day and all night with never a rest.

Monday 23 May – Thursday, 3 June [1938]. We started out early on our journey to Epila, leaving about 7 o'clock ... I drove all the way as we were in a hurry, and if anyone is going to break the car it is simplest it should be me. We had to be towed by the ambulance to start her, but once going she roared along in good form making a colossal row with her burst exhaust which was tied up with a piece of wire. We made record time and reached Zaragoza at 12.45 and Epila in time for lunch. It was grand to see Mama again. She and my brother John were sitting with Princess Bee and Prince Ali in the little garden when we pranced in absolutely filthy. As they had not expected us till the next day they were all very surprised. I was rather ashamed of my dirty uniform stained from head to toe, no make-up and my hair long and untidy, but Mama did not seem to mind a bit. She was looking so clean and cool and elegant in a smart dress and a white straw hat with a big diamond brooch in it. It seems all out of place to see anyone so clean and smart here, and it seems even odder that the people should be Mama and John. They stayed till Saturday which seemed a very short time. We always spent the day at Epila and usually I went back to Zaragoza where I shared a room with Mama for the night in the Grand Hotel. We were very idle and happy and did not do anything. Mama brought me letters from the family, lots of gossip and my press cuttings which were a hoot. Headlines and talk of Escatrón, and about my courage etc. In the mornings Mama and I would have breakfast in bed. She told me all the family gossip and London scandal. I told her all about what I had been doing and what it was like and the sort of work and general mess, until to my great surprise Mama begged me to stop telling her so many horrors or she would feel ill. It is evidently quite true that one gets so used to it all that one forgets what a normal idea of a horror is. Our days in Epila were peaceful and pleasantly idle. Sometimes we stayed to dinner and sometimes we dined in Zaragoza where I met Peter Kemp, the good-looking Englishman I once saw in Salamanca ages ago. He is now an 'alferez' in the Legion. He took me out to dinner one night. We dined at a strange little restaurant behind the cathedral of the Pilar and above a garage. I was the only female there, and it was full of Moors and a variety of soldiers. We finally got back to the hotel at about 12 o'clock and sat drinking until 1 o'clock. Peter told me a very sad tale illustrating the sadism of his colonel. Evidently one day an Englishman passed over to them from the Reds. Peter was sent to talk to him and found out that he was a sailor. His story was that he had gone on shore in Valencia and got tight. The next thing he remembered was being taken up to the front in a lorry. He could not escape, so at his first opportunity he had passed over in the hopes of getting sent home. Peter repeated this to the 'capitan' who said it sounded alright but he would have to ask the lieutenant-colonel about setting the man free. The 'terriente coronel' said it was OK by him but Peter would have to ask the colonel. Before he was half way through the story the colonel just said, 'Shoot him.' Peter sort of gaped and the colonel got angry and said, 'What is more, shoot him yourself or I will have you shot.' He even sent an officer after Peter to see that he did so, with orders to shoot him if not. So Peter led his Englishman off into the countryside. The man realized what was happening and asked if he was going to be shot, so Peter said yes. The man just answered 'Gee, that's tough.' Then Peter said if he wanted to die properly he was to walk quietly away in front of him. So the man shook hands with Peter, said 'Thanks anyhow', turned round and walked away and was duly shot. A nasty thing to have to do. Having power, especially over human lives, seems to go to people's heads and make them horrible almost always.

Pip entered Madrid on 28 March 1939, the day after the Nationalist troops occupied it. 'After the initial euphoria of victory a generalised depression set in. Pip, run down and ill, shared this depression in an acute form.'

We entered Madrid through the famous Ciudad Universitaria along a road built up ten or twelve feet high on either side like a trench. The view of Madrid from there was a waste land. Not a house standing, one mass of ruins. From there on there were enormous numbers of cars and lorries and troops, and we had to crawl along. The people of Madrid were pouring out, shouting and jumping on the running board, begging for food, cigarettes, anything ... The fortifications were unbelievable. Line after line of barricades of brick with loopholes all along for machine guns. It would have been utterly impossible to have taken Madrid by force except by completely destroying it and with great losses. The enthusiasm was unbelievable, a thing I shall never forget in my life. Flags and shawls and sheets hanging from every window and the streets filled with people shouting themselves hoarse and waving and saluting ... As long as I live, I shall never forget my first day in Madrid. It has been wonderful, incredibly happy and exciting, and at the same time terribly sad.

The Turn of the Years

The Seasons' Course

REYNOLDS STONE

As Old as the Century

V. S. PRITCHETT

Jacket illustration (by Reynolds Stone) and border red-brown, type black, cream background. Actual size. This was the first of a successful trio of short small-format cased books (designed by Humphrey Stone). See overleaf for the other two.

Sailing through China

PAUL THEROUX

Illustrated by

PATRICK PROCKTOR

Jacket illustration (by Patrick Procktor) and border red-brown, type black, cream background. Actual size.

PATAGONIA
REVISITED

BRUCE CHATWIN AND
PAUL THEROUX

Illustrated by
KYFFIN WILLIAMS

Jacket illustration (by Kyffin Williams) and border dark red-brown, type black, cream background. Actual size.

Bruce Shand

PREVIOUS ENGAGEMENTS

❧

This is a graphic, spirited, generous book that steals up on you and fills you with admiration for its author. Bruce Shand had been commissioned from Sandhurst into the 12th Lancers, an armoured car regiment, just before the Second World War, and took part in the fighting in France and Belgium before Dunkirk, then in the Western Desert, where he was taken prisoner.

The hazards and privations are stoically underplayed. They have 'an unpleasant time' in Furnes, a 'rather arduous' journey to La Penne. Just when they are about to take their place in the embarkation queue, they have to make an eight-mile trek along the sand to Dunkirk: 'under considerable bombing and a hot sun' it was 'really rather trying'. I bet it was.

The next day was spent in watching the reactions of the Belgians after they had ceased fighting. We now had only two troops left in the squadron, each of two cars, and we were kept very busy. I had to go off on a long trip to Roulers and Thourout and I found all the Belgians very uncommunicative. In the former place I had a discussion with the burgomaster who kept breaking into Flemish, which made conversation very difficult, and pointing at the statue of Nurse Cavell which adorns the centre of that town. Finally he made me the symbolic gift of an apple and I was left in some doubt of the whole affair ... I began to have less and less idea of what was happening – save that the Germans were doing rather well.

Our last two days as an active unit were spent in some very involved operations round Furnes and Dixmude, blowing up bridges over the Albert Canal and its tributary arms. At a village called

Schoorbacke I was responsible for the destruction of an enormous iron swing bridge. I was told this was mined and to hurry up. There was a French Sapper sergeant in charge who refused to blow it up or divulge where the fuses were, despite my assurance of the imminent approach of the enemy – which I knew, this time, for certain. Other bridges on my right and left were going up with encouraging explosions and I was peremptorily asked what I was doing. A brandished revolver and my entire stock of French invective had no effect on my friend and he only operated after I had been compelled to use third degree methods on him. It was hardly the way to treat one's ally; but the bridge disintegrated with the most stupendous noise and bits of it continued falling for some time. Luckily it had been mined properly and it completely disappeared. Only a few minutes later German armoured cars and tanks appeared on the opposite bank and under their spirited fire we withdrew.

That night (28–29 May) we had an unpleasant time in Furnes and the 29th saw most of the regiment on the edge of the Dunkirk perimeter. About midday we withdrew again. I got landed with the job of controlling traffic and sorting French and British into separate streams, which was exasperating work under a considerable aerial bombardment. In the evening the remainder of the squadron concentrated and a little later we received orders to destroy our vehicles. This we did by firing anti-tank bullets into the engines and then pushing the cars into one of the canals. We then marched off with our weapons to a field where we met the remainder of the regiment and the transport. We had some food and collected what kit we could carry and managed to get a comparatively good night's sleep which was sorely needed. Before dawn we were marching off to the seaside town of La Panne, leaving our lorries and spare luggage blazing behind us.

The journey to La Panne was rather arduous as we had a lot of arms and ammunition to carry and most of the men were still very tired. They played up wonderfully and we reached the town by midday. A very exhausting twenty-four hours followed as the regiment was made responsible for policing the beach and assisting in embarkation. Three jetties had been formed of lorries which were driven out into the sea and from the ends of these men were put into rowing boats which took them out to the vessels lying in deeper water. Each squadron had a jetty to look after and we worked, by shifts, until noon of the 31st. Most of the night was spent in getting off walking wounded; by dawn we were embarking ordinary personnel. For the most part discipline was excellent though there were one or two cases which brought little credit to the British Army. There was practically continuous bombing but we had a good anti-aircraft barrage, both from the shore and from destroyers, and I saw quite a few of the enemy shot down.

For our embarkation duties all of our officers were made ESOs (embarkation staff officers) and we were given powers to regulate the flow of troops. I think most of us managed to extract a lot of amusement out of a painful situation, by retarding the somewhat headlong rush of one or two staff officers whose duties apparently required their immediate presence in England ...

At midday on 31 May we were relieved by troops of General Alexander's 1st Division and prepared to take our place in the embarkation queue. Unfortunately the Germans chose that moment to start shelling La Panne, causing some casualties among the ships, and the Navy rightly decided to discontinue taking off troops there. We were therefore ordered to march to Dunkirk where apparently there was a 'chance' of getting a passage home. It was a trek of some eight miles along the sand and was really rather trying under considerable bombing and a hot sun. We adopted 'artillery formation' (memories of OTC field days!) and escaped with only a couple of men wounded.

On the outskirts of Dunkirk we met the colonel who had, by some remarkable process, acquired shipping space on two or three cement ships. Into these we gradually embarked, the shorter men having a very watery time as we had to wade out a fair distance. By about 7 p.m. we had all left the shore in some kind of vessel and I then saw the colonel, still looking immaculate, entering a small boat.

I remember very little of the journey back. Someone gave me some rum and I went to sleep in a sort of wheel house, into which we thrust ourselves, although it was already full. I had terrible attacks of cramp during the night and Rupert Byass told me afterwards that I kept kicking some luckless Frenchman in the face and murmuring 'S'il vous plaît, monsieur ...' He also told me that the ship was commanded by a midshipman who looked about twelve, assisted by a boatswain aged eighty.

We landed at Margate around 10 a.m. on 1 June.

The 12th Lancers were posted to North Africa. In early November 1942, Bruce, now a twenty-five-year-old major (with an MC and bar), ran into trouble.

Suddenly I saw a large concourse of vehicles coming towards me along the escarpment, a mile or so away. There was every reason to suppose they were British but I stopped and looked through my glasses, though visibility was becoming worse every minute. Still believing them to be ours, I moved on a little closer to see better, at the same time dispersing the squadron so that it would be ready to act in case they were not.

Some of them also came nearer and before I knew what had happened my own car was being heavily engaged with fire. Something like a whiplash stung my cheek, and Sergeant Francis beside me slumped to the bottom of the car with a large hole in his chest, killed instantly. I could hear all the other cars firing away hard. My mouth was full of blood but I managed to tell Corporal Plant, my imperturbable driver, to turn the car around. I also tried to talk on the wireless but it had become dislocated.

The car started to move but something hit it a tremendous blow, and I saw poor Plant subside over his wheel. A second later the car began to burn. Crawling forward I found that Plant was dead, and I prepared to leave the vehicle. I got through the top, jumped down and sheltered under the leeward side. Firing was still going on around me and from the remainder of the squadron.

I think I must have had a few minutes' blackout as I next remember

Edward's car approaching, with him shouting 'Jump on.' I managed to clamber on and hung rather precariously onto his hand as we began to move. It was then that I was hit in the knee, and in the sudden shock I let go, although he tried to hold me. I do not remember hitting the ground. A buzz of German voices greeted my return to consciousness.

He was shipped from Derna to the Piraeus, then installed in the Sismanoglion hospital in Athens.

Within a day or two I fell into trouble quite undeservedly. All hospitals, especially military ones, have to endure a grand tour of inspection by the chief doctor and his myrmidons, but in this German one the progress became almost majestic. Never have I seen so many hangers-on as followed the Oberst Arzt. Teutonic discipline demanded that one should lie to attention, on one's back with the arms on top of the sheets. Unaware of this regulation I suppose I was in a more comfortable and dégagé attitude. Anyway, it was enough to unsettle the whole echelon. Notes were taken and a flush of excitement came to the cheeks of the ward sister, a lady of immense girth and stature.

That evening she arrived at my bedside with a reluctant Greek nurse propelling a trolley bearing all the paraphernalia of colonic irrigation. An enema adequate for an elephant, yards of rubber tubing and gallons of soapy water. I protested that I had no need of this service but the colonel had spoken and I was to reap the reward for my insolence. Schwester advanced the nozzle while the Greek nurse slowly paid out a few fathoms of hose. Then, just before the critical moment, the sirens sounded, the lights went out and we were in for an air raid.

Forgetting my splinted leg, I leapt out of bed, pursued by the sister with a spouting jet of water, the pressure of which would have played havoc with my poor intestines should 'completion' have been achieved. I managed to get behind the bed of the Australian pilot who, overjoyed at the situation, quoted ten to one against 'the old bitch' catching me with 'the bum gun'. I, meanwhile, pretended to feel faint and a sort of peace was patched up. The Greek nurse laughingly started to mop up a sea of soapsuds and the sister, who had technically carried out her orders, wrote to that effect in her report.

After a month or more Bruce was told he was to be transferred to Germany. The hospital train wound slowly up to Salonika, then through the Balkans. At Salzburg there was a long halt.

One vignette remains in my memory of Salzburg. On the opposite platform a few people were awaiting an incoming train, amongst them a very distinguished-looking man in a long smart overcoat with a fur collar. He was accompanied by a beautiful lady, presumably his wife, and, presumably also, their two sons. The elder, on crutches, had probably been discharged from the Army, his face still a mass of scars. The younger, a cadet, looked no more than sixteen and both he and his mother were unable to stop their tears. The sight of our train full of the detritus of war cannot have helped. They looked delightful, civilised people and I pray that the poor boy did not end up in Russia.

Suffering from jaundice, Bruce was deposited from the hospital train at Magdeburg in Prussia and taken to what appeared to have once been a music hall in the town, supervised by some cynical French doctors and full of sick and dying Russian prisoners.

The subaltern from the rifle regiment, who could now walk, again raised the question of escape. His eyes had a strange look and I was convinced that he was all but insane. He announced to me one evening that he was 'going out' that night. I pointed out that it was snowing like mad, he had no overcoat, no German and no knowledge of the topography of Magdeburg. Where was he making for? He answered none of these questions. I could foresee a nasty situation: he would attempt to break out and we should all be punished as accomplices.

We were lucky. A call came for a volunteer to give blood for a transfusion for a British pilot shot down and lying in another hospital. The rifleman's group was the right one, so I ordered him into this humane task, telling him to use the opportunity to see what his chances were outside. As he had to walk a couple of miles each way in the snow, under armed guard, his enthusiasm cooled quite considerably and we were able to keep him tolerably quiet thereafter.

From there Bruce was taken to Spangenburg, where he remained until almost the end of the war. With the Americans advancing rapidly towards the camp, the prisoners were moved out eastwards. During the night march Bruce and one or two others managed to remove themselves from the column and two days later finally made contact with the Americans.

Martyn Skinner

OLD RECTORY

❧

Martyn Skinner was a modest and retiring spirit, whom I very much liked. I met him in 1983 when I did a selection of his five long poems under the title 'Alms for Oblivion'. I had come across his 'Letters to Malaya', published in three volumes in 1940, which won the Hawthornden Prize and the Heinemann Award for Literature. Written in heroic couplets, it is a series of imaginary conversations between the poet, who farms in Oxfordshire, and a civil servant friend in Malaya. 'Two Colloquies' (1945) repeated this conversational form. Extracts from 'Old Rectory' appeared in the volume and I reissued the full text the following year. The other two long poems which featured in 'Alms for Oblivion', in necessarily very truncated form, were 'Sir Elfadore and Mabyna' (Martyn's first published work in 1935) and a vast and heroically unfashionable epic poem entitled 'The Return of Arthur', in the manner of 'Don Juan', in which King Arthur returns from Avilion to liberate England from the powers of darkness. (Don't get up your hopes.) John Betjeman, a champion of Martyn Skinner's work, found it 'an amazing piece of sustained, imaginative writing'.

'Old Rectory' is set in the wilderness of post-plague Somerset, after the world has been depopulated by the Porton Sneeze. The Prologue describes the incidence of the plague and the hermit movement that accompanied it. Two professional interviewers, Fossick and Baytre, with a friend, J. J. Ponder, visit a local hermit called Old Rectory. The subject matter of the interview is varied but the main topic is Old Rectory's explanation of why he became a hermit, and how he recovered a faith that had been largely discarded by the interviewers and their world. There is a degree of autobiography here:

after coming down from Oxford the author spent some years as a monastic recluse.

I'm not suggesting 'Old Rectory' is for everyone: certainly it's nothing to do with any contemporary poetic fashion. On the other hand, it's technically skilful, allusive and quirkily original. The Marie Antoinette couplet, for instance, is a typically pleasing conceit. And in the lines quoted about the haybox, he catches the 'bin ... in' rhyme in a deft yet idiosyncratic way.

OLD RECTORY
I wasn't heading for the uterus.
Rousseau and Wordsworth are my Jung and Freud.
The origin I wanted to discuss
Was love of nature ...
PONDER May I intervene?
Such love of nature, as we've learnt, has been
A strong inducement – now and then, perhaps,
The main inducement – in the current phase
Of hermiting. But in the build-up scene
When you first sought, before the world's collapse,
Your haven, in those well-developed days
Exactly what did love of nature mean?
BAYTRE
It meant the love of countryside – excuse
My cutting in – by those who hungered still
To keep its precious scan, its cherished views
Unscathed, but lacked the vision and the will
To make the one essential sacrifice,
That is, to limit or forgo the use
Of gadgets that gave rise to ugliness,
Their workthings and their playthings – feebly loth
To drive one mile or turn one knob the less,
In hopes to have their cake and eat it too,
And serve god-Pan and Mammon-pylon both.
Result: the crumbled cake, the pyloned view.

Instead of countryside, an in-between
Of *rus in urbe* – greenbelt pastoral
With earshot traffic – and encroaching *urbs*
In rure – lanes with passing-bays and kerbs,
And scarlet kiosk on the village green,
And cottage shop's refrigerating hum,
And strip-lit smithy where the hunters come
On wheels – can you associate this all –
Modcons and love-of-nature compromise
With Wordsworth's creed and haunting waterfall?

OLD RECTORY

No more than, say, mastitis and the vet
With dairymaiding Marie Antoinette –
But ...

BAYTRE

Then your hermitage – was that some haunt
Deep valley-tucked, but handy for the jaunt
To town? Arcadian and undisturbed,
Yet up-to-date; beneath the blacksmith's latch
The locksmith's yale; the soil-pipe through the thatch,
And tell-tale grid upon the Tudor stack,
And tell-tale concrete drive-in to the back;
And where the view was, past a gnarled and fey
Peninsula of orchard trees that curbed
The frolic stream before it wound away,
Looped on black pole behind black pole behind
Black pole, the interloping wires that lined
Its long meanderings and didn't wind.

OLD RECTORY

You take one back to foregone days – to what
Might well have been some Georgian poet's cot,
Dorking or Ditchling – well, it wasn't mine.
My cottage shell, untenanted and tied
And due for demolition, stayed outside
– Though on the village outskirts – pipe and line.

I had its slates made waterproof, and then
Adding to what was required to make it fit
For human occupancy, and remit
The demolition order, in my cell
I settled down, like Jung at Bollingen,
To seek the treasure spurned by modern men,
Simplicity; earth's water from a well,
Warmth from a wood, a garden and a goat
(Your words; it's by telepathy I quote).

BAYTRE

At least you were consistent – had the sense
To see that if you loathed the consequence
The obvious remedy was to abstain
From causing it, by use of switch and main
And gadgetry and teletry.

OLD RECTORY A glutton

(You think) for abstinence, a Puritan
Troubled by scenic misdemeanours. No,
That mode of life was based on preference,
Not negative revulsion. I preferred
To any bulb or Belling instancy
My candles, kindly to the reading eyes,
That blended with instead of blotting out
The fireside's flicker to the further wall –
A simple blessing in a simple room,
Emblazoning its bareness. And I loved
To watch the four-cupped wrought-iron candlestick
Wax blond with tallow – kindling for the grate.
In the same way I would not have foregone
For all the taps in Chromia, the chore
That took me on dark mornings to the well,
This side or that of dawn, and as with crank
And creak of its old windlass I would haul
Up from a depth that made the very drips
Reverberate my climbing bucket clear,

Sometimes I'd glimpse, reflected in its load,
What seemed a silver minnow, the thin moon;
Or day's first cloud, a fluctuating rose.
Simple, inestimable. And I loved
The cheese I'd milked, the fire I'd sawn, the stew
I'd planted; loved the routine of a life
Shaped by such tasks, and worn into a gloss
By daily iteration – the same kind
Of homely patina that use had given
My shiny-handled spade. I loved as well
The indispensable, familiar few
Chattels I owned; on floor or shelf or hook
The landmarks of my indoor scenery,
Jug, skillet, basket, bowl, the haybox even ...
PONDER
Haybox? What's that?
OLD RECTORY ... ... An insulated bin
Or storage heater, where a boiling stew,
Once sealed, continued all night cooking in.
PONDER
A simple gadget – did Jung have one too?
FOSSICK
We're drifting from the point. This country zest,
This love of nature which you then possessed
And which first prompted you to hermitize –
Tell us, how did it differ from that tame
Fervour – Bay's Pan-and-pylon compromise –
That love of nature later on became?
OLD RECTORY
It was possession in a different sense –
I was possessed by it. For, suburb-bred,
I had a pavement boyhood. Larks for me
Were pranks, not birds. The apple-blossom's tinge
I never noticed; nor the change of sky
(The hoarding's change I did) except when clouds

Threatened a game of tennis, later golf.
(How far those pastimes make past times recede;
Remote as stoolball seems a stymie now.)
My walks were shopwards, past the numbered gates
Of parlour-like front-gardens, privet-walled,
Down to the Broadway's fascia-fascination.
Summer meant longer days, and little else;
And when day switched to night, the evening star
Had no clear call for me; such things I missed,
And even puberty did not assist.
And when in manhood I became aware,
Belatedly and fervently aware
Of nature's loveliness, it was as if
I saw with the same eyes, but different sight,
Myself the convert, a converted world.
For if small things may be compared with great,
A country lane was my Damascus Road.

Lavinia Smiley

A NICE CLEAN PLATE

❧

Lavinia Smiley's 'A Nice Clean Plate: Recollections 1919–1931', published in 1981, was an unusual quirky memoir of great charm. Lavinia was one of the three children of Clive Pearson, Lord Cowdray's younger brother, and her childhood was one of extreme affluence. What gave her book an unusual twist was her diffident attitude towards what some would have seen as her considerable advantages. I wrote in an obituary of her in the 'Sunday Telegraph': 'With the Pearson breadwinners in overslice, and with old Lady Cowdray, that doyenne of social consolidation, ordering Dunecht tweed by the mile, there were certainly aspects of Lavinia's start in life almost perversely at variance with her innate pessimism and besetting diffidence.' The book's opening sentence gives a taste of what is to follow: 'What made us unusual was our sense of anxiety, and our awareness of impending doom.'

I was nearly always sick. We were sick a great deal. It was brought on not only by being driven about in large yellow Rolls-Royces but also by any kind of emotion.

We were once taken to a performance of Longfellow's 'Hiawatha' in the Albert Hall, where our grandmother had a box, and when Famine came walking down on to the stage, with full supporting chorus, we were all three so overcome that we had to be hurried out. We were walked round and round the Albert Memorial, on a cold grey afternoon, to recover. Eventually the chauffeur and the yellow Rolls-Royce arrived to drive us home again, crestfallen and ashamed.

We had a seedy canary called Joey whose cage hung in the nursery

RECOLLECTIONS
1919–1931

LAVINIA SMILEY

Humphrey Stone's title page for 'A Nice Clean Plate'.

window. He was an unsatisfactory pet whose destiny went wrong – he was supposed to go to the actress Gladys Cooper, then called *Lady* Pearson, and in confusion with *Mrs* Pearson, my mother, he got delivered to the wrong house. By the time the mistake was discovered we had unpacked him and become fond of him (or so we said), and it seemed a miracle that we were allowed to keep him.

Our pocket money for years was five shillings a month and we were taken, by special arrangement, to William Deacon's Bank at No 9 Pall Mall to collect it. A serious man in a black coat would ask us how we would like our money. It took us ages to decide. Dione was sometimes allowed to sit up on the counter so that she could see him shovelling the coins into three little brown paper bags. She quite often chose to have hers in pennies or halfpennies, whereas Veronica and I chose the more sophisticated coinage of sixpences or threepenny bits – in those days silver – or even just five straight shillings. Now and again Veronica would boldly have just two half-crowns. The serious cashier must have known my father as he never allowed even the flicker of a smile to cross his face during these lengthy transactions.

We had to account for every penny spent, each in a tall thin red marbled account book. Every so often there would be consternation bordering on panic when word came that my father was coming up to 'do the accounts'. He very seldom came anywhere near the nursery and we saw very little of him, as he got home from the office after we had gone to bed, which made it doubly alarming. We would sit by the nursery table with him, very seriously, while he took us book by book. The entries were few, consisting mostly of 'Present for Veronica', 'Pencil Sharpener', Put in box for Waifs and Strays', or 'Present for Nanny'. It was a great relief when, having made us do the addition and subtraction, which almost never balanced, he would say: 'Then let us put "Unaccounted for – 8 1/2d" and that will make it all come right.'

My grandfather had made a large fortune. I just remember him as the kindest and gentlest of men. My grandmother was clearly the perfect helpmeet for him. She was immensely capable, a wonderful organiser, blessed with boundless vitality, hard-working, benevolent, ambitious, and made everything as grand as possible. We were perhaps justified in finding her absolutely terrifying. She was one of a large family of well-to-do Yorkshire Casses. Her father, Sir John Cass, was at one time Mayor of Bradford, and she saw herself as founding a dynasty. This could explain why she decided quite early on in her married life that certain members of her family – and indeed of her husband's – must be dropped, since they would not be able readily to climb to the heights she planned. This dropping process was done with a ruthlessness which may have appalled plants more sensitive than herself: everything was done for the advancement and advantage of her own immediate family. She was known by all her descendants as 'Gan'. She was short and stocky, and wore pince-nez.

The second part of our summer holidays was spent at Dunecht.

The excitement about the journey to Scotland was intense. Mr Petre would drive us to King's Cross Station and we would fill almost a whole carriage of first-class sleepers, and were allowed to walk along to look at the engine, steaming furiously, before being put to bed.

Then there was the struggle to be awake when going over the Forth Bridge. It was like going into a new world.

For many years all the taxis waiting at Aberdeen Station were Rolls-Royces – demoted from a more gracious castle life among the lairds, I suppose – and in one (or two) of them we would be driven the fifteen miles through rolling farmland to Dunecht.

There would be other guests, with dogs and guns and fishing rods; and on arrival that first breakfast – porridge with the thickest cream, and eggs and bacon and sausages, and herrings in oatmeal, and heather honey spread on baps – was so marvellous that one would momentarily forget the awaiting ordeal of being presented to Gan. Strains of the bagpipes came drifting in at the windows. I suppose the piper played for about an hour each morning, walking slowly between the herbaceous borders and then round and round the courtyard.

Gan would gather the whole clan around her during part of August and September. In addition to her sons, daughter, and daughters-in-law there would be a host of Old Friends and Bright Young Things – suitable friends of Yoskyl, Nancy, John and Angela, Brenda, Judy and Joan. Also of course Aunts Gertie and Maggie.

When even the great house of Dunecht was full, we four youngest grandchildren had the good luck to be put – with our own retainers – in a granite villa in the park (known in Scotland as the policies) called Craig-na-Loich.

Church was a great thing on those Scottish holidays. And clergymen. There was Bishop Browne, who stayed for long periods writing a book called 'Antiquities in the Neighbourhood of Dunecht', in due course suitably bound in purple. (I believe he was rather a worldly bishop and left Mrs Browne and all the little Brownes at home for months at a time while he basked in splendour.) In addition to the Bishop, Gan imported for the Season a gentle Yorkshire vicar, the Rev. Harold Anson, to conduct services in the large chapel attached to the house, to which some of the local gentry also came.

My mother told me that poor Mr Anson was dreadfully embarrassed when Gan announced that, for reasons of hygiene, instead of a Communion cup it would be preferable to have small individual glasses. He knew that this would not be acceptable in the eyes of the Church, but found it very difficult to disagree with her on any point whatever. Perhaps the Bishop dared to put his foot down as the little glasses were never used.

Lavinia's other books were five picture books for children and 'The Frasers of Castle Fraser'. To quote the obituary again, 'she had a knack for catching a fairly simple image in an original and comic way, with a controlled eccentricity of line that was sometimes extraordinarily pleasing. Her children's books exemplified this talent. 'Robin in Danger' and 'Hugh the Dragon Killer', her first two picture books, were published by Faber in 1956. Twenty years later Michael Russell republished these with three fresh titles, 'William and the Wolf', 'Clive to the Rescue' and 'Buster's Holiday' ... Her last published work was 'The Frasers of Castle Fraser' (1988), the product of long and happy hours in the muniment room at the Smileys' Aberdeenshire home. It was a book of studious enthusiasm, and radiated the pleasure that had gone into making it.'

Line drawing of Parham by Lavinia Smiley from 'A Nice Clean Plate'. This was the Sussex house acquired and restored by her father.

Reinhard Spitzy

HOW WE SQUANDERED THE REICH

❧

It was Richard Lamb, whose 'The Ghosts of Peace 1935–1945' I had published in 1987, who put me in touch with Reinhard Spitzy. His book had had a considerable success in Germany and he was taking a robust line with a publisher over here who wanted him to make alterations. The translation, by Geoff Waddington, an academic at Leeds, was particularly good; some of the views expressed might raise eyebrows, but 'sui generis' I thought would cover it – after all, this was someone who had been committed to the Nazi movement up until Munich, had served in Ribbentrop's London embassy, had accompanied Hitler on the Anschluss and had personally encountered all the Nazi top brass. Besides, some of the anecdotal material was extraordinary. Most interesting perhaps were its insights into why Hitler and the Nazis were so attractive. We went ahead. Taki in his High Life column in the 'Spectator' described it encouragingly as 'the best book ever'. Barry Humphries, in his Books of the Year selection in the 'Sunday Telegraph', found it a 'riveting chronicle', that described 'with convincing candour the author's love affair with the Führer and his disenchantment'.

Reinhard's account of his service in London with Ribbentrop ('Brickendrop') is at once comic and disturbing.

My main job was to act as the chief's 'shadow'. I had to be at his disposal from early morning to late at night. This was both irritating and arduous, but it had its advantages in that the Ribbentrops always put on an excellent spread. Moreover, as I frequently had to accompany the chief to the Foreign Office, I had to dress accordingly, and was thus instructed to acquire a splendid wardrobe from Lesley and Roberts at the expense of the German government. The chief and I, dressed like twins and both wearing bowler hats, would stride together through the dark corridors of Whitehall to the Ambassadors' waiting room, whence he would be collected by Halifax, Henderson, Chamberlain or Eden. On such occasions I would be introduced to the British statesmen and Ribbentrop always made a point of describing me as his 'private secretary'. This was rather pleasing, since 'private secretary' is not an entirely accurate translation of our *Privatsekretär*, and is, in fact, something of an overstatement ... The British statesmen were more friendly towards me with each meeting and sometimes even honoured me with a few polite words. Whenever Ribbentrop strutted down the corridors like a peacock, with his head arched and his hands pressed into the small of his back, it was a miracle that he didn't fall over backwards. It was marvellously entertaining to watch him indulge in such pretensions, and the Foreign Office officials grinned at me with a mixture of sympathy and amusement as we passed.

The Nuremberg rally of September 1937 was Nazism at its most seductive.

I enjoyed the Nuremberg rally with my heart and soul, and was seized by as much idealism as it is possible for a young man to possess. Many of the finer details impressed me, including the time when three gliders, flying in tight formation, made an amazing coordinated landing directly in front of the Führer's rostrum. The organization and stage management was simply flawless, and the degree of imagination and inventiveness that had gone into the planning of the whole occasion was almost miraculous.

'Shortly after the Italians had conquered Abyssinia Mussolini had announced that he wished to pay a visit to Germany as a sign of his gratitude.'

The high point of the visit was undoubtedly the huge meeting at the Maifeld, the former Reich sports stadium which had been constructed for the 1936 Olympiad. No less than 650,000 people were due to turn out, of whom only a few were spectators in the ordinary sense of the word. The vast majority consisted of detachments of men lined up side by side in tight formation like pieces on a chessboard. It had been intended to crown the festivities by recreating the sensational 'cathedral of light' effect which had made such an impression recently in Nuremberg. Unfortunately, however, the rain, fog and clouds conspired to thwart the plan, and, instead of the dramatic spectacle which had been achieved at the party rally, the searchlight beams simply highlighted a huge 'pea souper' overhead.

The 'historic event' finally came to a terrific climax in a crescendo of fanfares, singing, trumpets and drums. Everything had been calculated down to the last detail, apart, that is, from the massive rush for shelter which took place as soon as the final act had been solemnly concluded. All of a sudden thousands upon thousands of people, already soaked to the skin, began making their way in disorderly throngs towards the exits. Before long it became evident that the iron discipline, which up to this point had been such a marked feature of the entire event, was on the verge of total collapse. There was yet more commotion in the car park where Frau von Ribbentrop had managed to get herself caught up and had been unable to move either forwards or backwards. One can imagine just how annoyed she was at having missed everything.

Nevertheless, the departure of the Führer and the Duce passed off smoothly and without incident. They made their way to the exit, closely pursued by their immediate entourages, seated themselves in their open-top Mercedes and roared off into the night. It was quite a different story as far as everybody else was concerned. At first people tried to do things by the book and maintain at least a semblance of protocol, but before long it developed into a free for all with each person pushing and fighting his way as fast as he could down staircases and through gangways towards the cars in a desperate effort to keep up with the two leaders. In theory this was laudable; in practice, however, completely impossible. Marshal Badoglio, the illustrious conqueror of Abyssinia, almost tumbled down a flight of stairs, and it was only with some difficulty that he was prevented from being trampled underfoot by the decorated masses following close on his heels. Military attachés and diplomats lost their decorations and ceremonial sashes, and in the chaos I inevitably became separated from the chief and my other colleagues. By this time it was absolutely pouring down, and dignitaries were repeatedly knocked to the floor and trudged on by lesser mortals. There was now no trace of the stirring marching music or trumpets, just one almighty racket. Thousands of people had congregated at the entrance to the underground and, as we secretly heard later, over twenty lost their lives in the ensuing crush. The famous German military was for once completely powerless, its units having totally fallen apart in the confusion.

Having already lost my cape, and with my clothes torn and dishevelled, I forced my way through to the car park where I commandeered the first decent vehicle I came across. This belonged to some lowly party boss, and, bellowing at the top of my voice and pointing to who I was and for whom I worked, I immediately forced him to hand it over. Later that night I arrived back in the centre of town where the 'world historical' drama continued to be played out. The Duce and the Führer had by now made their way to the city centre down the East-West Axis, which had been transformed into a magnificent boulevard, fit for the grandest of parades, bedecked with flags and steaming pans of pitch hoisted high on pylons. The rain was teeming down, and although both leaders were pleased by the acclamation of the crowds, they were drenched and hoarse after their exertions at the Maifeld. Understandably the Führer wished to accompany Mussolini personally to the quarters where he was to reside for the duration of his visit, the imposing palace of the former Crown Princes and Reich Presidents in the Wilhelmstrasse. During their journey back from the stadium Mussolini, who could speak some German, had already complained a little of the cold and the rain, and had also remarked that he could feel a sore throat coming on.

His Bedraggled Excellency was deposited at his extravagantly prepared apartment to be dealt a nasty shock. No hot water, no central heating. His mood and his faith in German efficiency were said to have hit an all time low. How had it happened?

According to a decree dating back to the early years of the Prussian Ministry of the Interior, a decree which was later confirmed by the thrifty Reich President von Hindenburg, all central heating in official buildings, such as the palace in which Mussolini was staying, was to be turned off at five o'clock in the afternoon. Consequently, the responsible palace official, acting in the true Prussian tradition of obedience, had dutifully obeyed the regulations and flicked the switch at five o'clock on the dot. Unfortunately no one had reckoned with a bureaucrat who would abide by the regulations to the letter. Embarrassingly, it had to be the leader of Fascist Italy who had been inconvenienced by such evident devotion to duty, with the result that the hapless official was forced to spend several harrowing hours at Gestapo headquarters. It was clear that no charges could be brought against him, however, and, as far as I know, he was released within a few days after Goering intervened on his behalf.

Now it was Hitler's turn to visit Mussolini.

No sooner had I arrived back in Berlin than I became caught up in the turbulent and extensive preparations which were then under way for Hitler's forthcoming visit to Italy [1938] ...

Incredible as it may seem, new uniforms appeared to be the most pressing issue of the moment. Ribbentrop had several versions of a new diplomatic uniform designed. Assuming the role of male model, I was sent to parade the various designs before Hitler, who found the whole affair quite tedious. The diplomatic uniform finally emerged as a cross between the Navy and Army designs, with rank being indicated by a series of stripes on the sleeves rather than insignia on the collar patches. A huge row erupted when it was discovered that other Ministers wished to use the same design for their own officials.

The elite diplomatic uniform, so laboriously created by Herr and Frau von Ribbentrop, was thus in danger of being degraded to the level of that worn by forestry and agricultural officials. Such was the Ribbentrops' tenacity, however, that they eventually succeeded in fending off this unwelcome danger. In fact, only the officials from the Presidential Chancellery were permitted to use our design with the result that their chief, State Secretary Meissner, had the same number of stripes embroidered on his sleeves as Ribbentrop had on his. Thereupon Ribbentrop quickly added another to his own outfit. In order to prevent the competition developing to the ludicrous point where the stripes reached all the way up to the shoulders, Ribbentrop later decided that the Foreign Minister should have his own special insignia, a globe crowned with laurels. Consequently the number of stripes on the sleeves of his jacket was reduced.

Sartorial problems did not end there. On the Roman visit

... we had vacated our box in the theatre and were preparing to take part in the military parade which had been planned for that night. We were all much taken aback to see that Hitler, who was nervously fiddling with his moustache, had turned up in top hat and tails. He did not cut an impressive figure in such attire, and looked rather like a cross between a head waiter and a chimney sweep. Something dreadful must have happened. A gaffe of such proportions must surely have been planned in advance by reactionary elements of the Italian Protocol Department. The programme had stated explicitly that following the opera performance the Führer would be able to use one of the dressing rooms for a full twenty minutes before the military parade got under way. When the time came, however, one of the adjutants, Admiral Count Thaon de Revel, had approached Hitler in a rather brusque manner and explained to him with some firmness: 'Your Excellency, because of numerous delays the programme is running behind schedule. I regret to say it will no longer be possible for Your Excellency to change. The troops are already marching. We would therefore be greatly obliged if Your Excellency would take part in the parade dressed as you are now.' Hitler must have been incensed, but he accepted the explanation and was polite enough not to let his true feelings show. The lengthy march past which followed must have been sheer torture for him. As a former front-line soldier he absolutely loathed the sight of top hats and tailcoats at military functions, Moreover, he knew he was no Adonis. This conspiracy, engineered by the court lackeys, was not to be without consequence.

Reinhard, engaged to an English girl (an engagement which, with the onset of war, had to be broken), was becoming increasingly disillusioned.

Immediately after the [Munich] conference I too began to lose heart as a result of a personal experience which made a profound and lasting impression upon me. Chamberlain had asked Hitler if it would be possible to pay him a further visit for the purpose of obtaining his signature to a document which stated – in fairly general terms – that Britain and Germany were resolved to co-operate towards the peaceful resolution of future international problems. Hitler, who was taken completely by surprise, agreed to sign the statement, but did so with little enthusiasm. After all, he could hardly refuse. Shortly afterwards Hitler and Ribbentrop paid another short visit to the Führerbau. As they were leaving the building I was following a little distance behind them when I overheard Ribbentrop making derisory remarks about the Munich Agreement, and in particular about Chamberlain's 'peace declaration'. To my absolute horror Hitler responded in a half-whisper: 'Oh, don't take it all so seriously. That piece of paper is of no significance whatsoever.'

During the war, serving in Admiral Canaris's Abwehr, Reinhard played an active part in the resistance movement. Transferred to Spain, he had a secret meeting with Allen Dulles to explore the possibilities of peace negotiations with the West. After a spell in South America after the war, he returned in 1957 to Austria, where he still lives.

Freya Stark

LETTERS: VOLUMES 1–8

edited by Lucy Moorehead (1–6)
and Caroline Moorehead (7–8)

❧

I've touched on my dealings with Freya Stark in the Introduction. Her old friend and publisher, Jock Murray, had opposed her plan to publish the whole corpus of letters. I was just getting going, there was some money in Switzerland to underpin the financial risk, and Freya was determined to do it anyway. In the event Jock Murray couldn't have been more friendly and helpful, so I didn't feel party to any disharmony. And after we'd completed the eight-volume marathon, Murray's (politely 'in association with Michael Russell') published a single volume of Selected Letters, 'Over the Rim of the World', edited by Caroline Moorehead. Which is really what they'd suggested all along. For all that there's something cumulatively impressive about our pantechnicon. We still sell the odd set. Patrick Leigh Fermor, writing in the 'Times Literary Supplement', shall have the last word: 'The most coherent, impressive and stimulating body of letters it is possible to imagine. Admirably edited ... beautifully produced.' Don't mind that.

To Venetia Buddicom, from Baghdad, 3 December 1932.

Last night I went to hear the 'Egyptian Nightingale', a singer called Umm Kalthum. She draws enormous crowds to a rather low-down hotel completely built of wood, on to whose floors and timber balconies the audience was casting lighted cigarettes with complete recklessness. Umm Kalthum was very modestly dressed in black, up to the chin and down to the wrists and ankles, with what looked like a French beret on one side of her head, and a rather nice determined little round face underneath. She had a row of singularly plain men in tarbushes on either side of her, ready to twang on lutes and other amusing instruments: they were making a few desultory noises, while Umm Kalthum dropped isolated notes at intervals, unrecognised by us as a tune until we heard the audience sigh with long 'ah's and 'oh's. I was glad to hear it: she had a good voice (all from the throat) and the beauty seems to consist in pouring as much emotion as you can into it, so that it is as near like actual sobbing as music possibly can be. But I should not care to hear it very often.

To Sir Sydney Cockerell, from Simla, 6 March 1943.

I have left Delhi, after three such happy weeks: my devotion to the Wavells much increased and the feeling that I was leaving real friends. It was pleasant too to talk about poetry rather than propaganda. Now I have spent £1,000 on a new car and all its appurtenances and am taking it all the way back across Baluchistan and Persia and hope to sell it for a large profit in Baghdad. If I don't, I don't care: I would any day *do* things than *have* things, and a journey like this is very alluring. An old friend in the RAF is I hope meeting me in Quetta (with a revolver). My only anxiety is the value of a car now; in Persia and Iraq new tyres are worth £170 each! It makes it worth robbing.

The Mogul has been a revelation of real loveliness and the civilised art of living; the British is most fascinating: so much good, and something so wrong. In the building I have come to the conclusion it is the want of spontaneity; nothing is done for *fun*; no one just thought he would like a grotto, a fountain, or a lattice and put it there. While assisting at an investiture in the great marble throne room I kept hearing in my head 'Nor in your marble *vault* shall sound my echoing song' – and perhaps that is what is wrong with all Official India. It seems to have preserved a Victorian rigidity, but without the Victorian passion behind it. And of course they take themselves seriously, which is always fatal. Even now, in most places, one feels our lack of training in formal courtesy. Here, for instance, none of the villagers ever say good day as they pass in a lonely footpath: I said so and they looked surprised, but coming back the same way, all greeted me delighted. The women here are *fantastic*: Kipling without a comma to add or alter, and quite frightful. But oh Sydney – the snowy hills! What a vision, quite unforgettable – the serenity of the Gods, peak after peak, a shining white barrier sea of steady waves hemming the north and east – even their names unknown. There is a map in the hall, it says 20,000 feet, 18,000 feet – belonging to the great Himalayan range. I told the Field Marshal I would not like my life over again, but I *did* feel when looking there this morning and remembering I am fifty years old that I should like to be young just to penetrate among them. (I have walked three hours today, which isn't bad for the first day at this height – but am all aches from my bruised back falling off a horse.)

You ask whether I would have liked my life different. I think not. The years at Dronero I regret, but what came before and after was all good and I feel that I have acquired my philosophy such as it is and that is what really matters. The object of life, if I were asked, I should say is to conquer fear: and 'perfect love casteth out fear'. One is only on the way, but at any rate it is something to know where the path leads that lies before you. I do regret now not being married: but not the marriages of those days I wrote to you about. The man with whom I would have been happy, and who cared, was killed by the Germans in Stuttgart in April 1939. *[This was Donald Lennox-Boyd.]* And now – I feel lonely, but I know it does not very much matter. Also I have so much love for which to be grateful or humble. In that I am spoiled above most people; and at least, I do value it at its worth.

Pedigree: my paternal grandfather died when my father was a little boy, so he is very vague. He was well off and lived at Torquay doing nothing as far as I know (but I may be wrong): *his* father or grandfather, also a Robert, was full of character and started a Non-Conformist sect and gave much trouble to the bishops of the West

Country: I have his picture in Asolo – a good bulldog sort of Cromwellian face. My mother's three sisters were all most temperamental and trying, always in straits for money. The eldest, Lily, married a rich American who died leaving her with a small income, three daughters, a lunatic son, and no capacity for living inside any income ...

It is nice to sit talking to you here in Simla, where I so little expected ever to find myself. One thing I have felt again very strongly today – that no *human* work ever moves me one fraction as deeply as does the sight of nature, but especially of mountains: only sometimes the Greeks, because in their holy places they have made themselves one with nature. The sight of these great giants has given me a sort of new breath of life today.

To her husband, Stewart Perowne, whom she had married the year before, on 7 November 1948, from Bernard Berenson's I Tatti.

At Asolo a frantic five days' wait for me to get packed and away. We had three days completely taken up with a visit from the Madonna of Fatima, which is a place in Portugal where she appeared and is now 'visiting her people' all over Europe. The dioceses send out a statue and from parish to parish it is handed on. Asolo went to receive her at the bridge of Pagnano on a very wet night, about 5,000 people with candles wrapped round with pink or green paper guards, under umbrellas. It was so wet I stayed and watched from La Mura where one could see the little lights and shiny umbrellas pouring like a Chinese print down the church steps while the loudspeaker chanted 'Vogliamo Iddio: il Nostro Re.' Then there were three days of visiting, the schools, the orphans, the hospital. An irreverent voice in the crowd said, 'How can we keep our wives at home, if the Madonna gads about at night?' The last of it was an evening procession past our house and down to Casella where the parish of S. Apollinaire came to fetch her. Every house in Asolo and all those on the hillside were illuminated; it was charming and touching. The baker stacked his bread with green ribands, and the fruitseller piled his apples and grapes with garlands, and people decorated little altars in their doorways and put the children's photographs with the holy pictures to be blessed in passing. Our house looked lovely as Checchi hung paper lanterns in the poplar trees, and candles and the four-beaked Florentine lamps in the windows, and a candle on every spike of the gate; so that Monsignore, when he came leading the procession like a conductor, stepped aside from the vanguard of rather haughty little boys he keep under his immediate eye, and stepped out to congratulate (very pleased at this Protestant tribute). We joined the procession for a little way so as to see it as it curved down the valley. It was immensely long, the Madonna fluttering blue and white on the people's shoulders, and a cash-box, white, with two gilt angels, carried before her, and a car with a huge loudspeaker just in front, with a strong young priest beside it, intoning into the microphone, 'Maria, ave; abbi di noi pieta.' The chants were taken up and the river of lights sparkled all down the valley. The whole way to the plain was lit with little glow-worms of candles along the walls, and the light just showed the black outline of the moving figures. It was so ancient, pagan, heartfelt, and spontaneous that one could not help being deeply moved. How you would have loved it; it seemed to be a thread of history, tying the little town to all its own past, so that the shops and streets and houses were still what they have always been, right back to their earliest foundations.

To Paul Scott, on the subject of W. P. Ker, Freya's godfather and an early influence: 20 May 1976.

So interested in your letter, but sorry that my beloved godfather didn't come through. Is it perhaps that the Scotch leave so much unsaid? He never did what someone said a gathering of bishops should have done: 'Ils ont perdu l'occasion de se taire.' I am sure you would have come through into the unseen country if you had known him; and he would have liked and talked to you, because you are interested in humanity as well as literature, and the inarticulate must after all have someone articulate for any conversation at all. W. P. knew fifteen languages and their literatures and an Italian friend once asked 'Does he speak in monosyllables in all of them?' But he talked to me, and many of his sayings I still remember, and so do many of his friends – did, I should say, for this was all long ago! Wavell too was no talker, and once told me that he would give almost anything for the capacity of a little 'drawing-room chitchat'.

From a letter to Jock Murray from Bodrum, 10 June 1976.

I am writing by moonlight: a little sunset comes into it, but it really is the moon, almost round, filling the bay. The place has become a little more elegant – blue cotton for the waiters – and naturally more expensive, but a warm welcome: kisses from the hostess and the washerwoman, the children two years taller and that climate of civilisation which goes down to the poorest and one seems to lose between the Mediterranean and the Celtic fringe of Dartmoor and Scotland. It was a marvellous drive up from Alanya: the mountains with clouds like fighting dragons, snow on the tallest; the Maeander showing its perfect valley-shape, gathered in a basin so wide you might call it a plateau, except for the high prison lines of the barriers that hem it; then gradually the valley forms (below the lake where the flute was invented), still very wide and lush, and every plant seeming to grow into a tree, and the river rolling down smooth and mostly invisible, carrying its history and with it the memories I took there twenty-four years ago. It all looks more prosperous now in spite of crisis, the industrial age coming with a natural Turkish untidiness that makes a ruin of a building just begun.

And finally a footnote from Volume Eight, nicely catching Freya's essence. There was a reference in the text to Miss Caton Thompson. The footnote explains:

The archaeologist whom F. S. had accompanied on a contentious expedition in the winter of 1937–8 in Southern Arabia. The letters for that period were somewhat acerbic on the subject of Miss Caton Thompson, and F. S.'s views seemed not to have mellowed over the years. Lucy Moorehead, making her plea for editorial restraint, added that Miss Caton Thompson was after all still alive. 'Typical,' F. S. replied.

Virginia Surtees

THE LADY LINCOLN SCANDAL

❧

In 1832 Lady Susan Hamilton, daughter of the 10th Duke of Hamilton (and granddaughter of William Beckford – hence our rather disingenuous original title of 'A Beckford Inheritance'), married Lord Lincoln, the Duke of Newcastle's heir. The marriage matured into a high-profile disaster. Sir Philip Magnus, reviewing the book in the 'Daily Telegraph', described it as 'Enthralling ... intensely interesting not merely as a dramatic tale of human passion and folly but also for the light which it throws upon manners, conduct and modes of thought and expression of a vanished patrician world.' That's it; the context is everything. And Virginia Surtees excels at the Victorian haut monde.

Here are the two Dukes in match-making mode. First the Duke of Newcastle, encumbered by debt, with ten children on his hands, to the Duke of Hamilton.

My Lord Duke, It has more than once appeared to me that your Grace's feelings & mine may probably coincide upon a subject which deeply interests us both. For myself, I can truly state that the subject is one of most distressing anxiety to me, on account of the very peculiar situation in which I am placed with regard to the females of my family, which makes it of the greatest importance for the others, as well as for themselves, that my eldest daughters should be desirably settled in life.

I will not disguise from your Grace that there is no young man in the country to whose charge I should so readily & confidently commit the happiness of my daughter as Lord Douglas [the Duke of Hamilton's heir] ...

I must throw myself upon your Grace's goodness to pardon what may appear to you to be an extraordinary step on my part; I would not, however, attempt to give encouragement to what I so anxiously desire, unless it met with your Grace's entire approbation. It is not Ld Douglas's situation & eminent prospects, but his character which prompts me to covet such an alliance ...

Of course. And the Duke of Hamilton replies:

It is most true, there is a sympathy of feeling between us. I am proud of it. Those very feelings that have induced your Grace to write to me distinguishing Douglas in the most flattering manner in which a parent could distinguish any young man, were operating upon my mind at the very same moment in regard to Lord Lincoln [the Newcastle heir]; & when your letter arrived, strange as the coincidence may appear, I had almost resolved, with equally good reasons, & upon a similar conviction to address your Grace in a similar strain.

I have an only daughter, the object of my tender affection & most anxious solicitude, & the proposal I had in contemplation to make was of the same nature with the one which I have just been honoured with from your Grace in so handsome a manner ...

The letter gave the Duke of Newcastle 'a new life & cheered my spirits ...'

Your Grace has only proposed to me what I would gladly accept. I presume that Lady Susan is all that may be looked for from a daughter of the Duchess of Hamilton – & that character, temper, & every female virtue have been deeply cultivated, that happiness from such an union must be next to certain ...

It didn't work out like that. Here is William Gladstone, a family friend, in the dual role of redeemer and private investigator, arriving in Como, where the pregnant Suzie and her lover Lord Walpole had taken the Villa Mancini.

Dramatis personae:

Mr Gladstone – Mr Gladstone
Suzie – Lady Lincoln
Lord Walpole – Suzie's lover
Trincavelli – Lord Walpole's valet
Catherine – Mrs Gladstone
Santi – courier
Job – maid

When Mr Gladstone reached Como on July 31st [1849], shortly after Lord Walpole had left it, he breakfasted, and then 'set about the sad purpose' of his visit, but 'somehow thinking Lord W was not here and feeling certain I should find Lady L, I was light-headed when I commenced my enquiries'. Learning from the police that Mrs Laurence lived at the Villa Mancini, he presented himself at the iron gate and sent in his card, handing it to the gardener's wife. She passed it on to Trincavelli who happened to be at hand and he carried it inside, giving it to Santi who took it upstairs to Suzie's room where he and Job were packing. The relief to Suzie must have been overwhelming. Instead of a husband on the doorstep, legally empowered to drag her back to England, here was Mr Gladstone whom she could refuse to see, and might elude during the night. She had probably little inclination to reason out the possibility of his following her, nor the strength, in the stifling heat, to form any other plan than that which had been concocted the previous night. The fact that she had been discovered after a year of reckless irresponsibility, and at the critical moment of impending confinement, was quite horrifying enough. She sent Santi down to the gate; Gladstone asked for Mrs Laurence and was told he could not see her; on enquiring 'in a rather marked manner' for the Countess of Lincoln, he was assured that no such person lived there.

It was now vitally important for Gladstone to ascertain the identity of Mrs Laurence, so settling himself in the courier's room, he addressed her a letter explaining that if she would allow him an interview he could account for the strangeness of his behaviour. With this letter (of which he made a copy) he enclosed that of his wife, brought with him from England, which dwelt on her affection for Suzie and gave a pathetic little description of the Lincolns' ten-year-old daughter, Susan ... She had heard with regret of Suzie's 'tumble' in Rome (the euphemism given for seclusion when pregnancy became too apparent), and with true ingenuousness hoped to hear of a happy recovery ...

In his letter to Catherine that evening Gladstone disclosed the one great overwhelming shock he had sustained in the knowledge of Suzie's condition, and admitted that learning 'this horror from the *laquais de place* who conducted me to the Villa, it threw me into such a tremor and palpitation that I could hardly write: for I am one of those who are always sufficiently shocked at other people's sins.'

Trincavelli was called to bring a candle for Gladstone to seal the letter which Santi then took with him. Gladstone's hope was that in writing to Mrs Laurence he was providing against the chance of his being mistaken, which 'morally, I felt sure I was not', while 'Lady Lincoln's desire to know something about her children might induce her to open the letter. I think I gave an intimation to that effect to the courier.' After ten minutes Santi returned with the letter from Mrs Gladstone, unopened, and a verbal message to the effect that Lady Lincoln was unknown to Mrs Laurence who could not see him on grounds of illness.

Returning to the hotel – for it was now afternoon – Gladstone, having failed to collect evidence of identity, felt obliged to write once again and was under the illusion that, by requesting, he would obtain a written reply and thereby recognize Suzie's handwriting. In this he was no luckier than in his earlier attempt.

Trincavelli meanwhile had not forgotten to fetch his master's passport from the police, where it had been given a visa for Switzerland. His next errand was to order three post horses to be sent up to the villa in the evening, and shortly before their arrival, while standing near the house, he saw to his surprise 'the English Gentleman' walking up and down the road before the gates. By the time the horses arrived and had entered the front court it was quite dark and Trincavelli lowered the lantern over the front door and lit it so that the carriage could be packed with the greatest speed. Gladstone meanwhile passed and repassed the gates. Santi came out of the house and handed Trincavelli a packet of letters addressed to Walpole to be given to him with his passport the next day, cautioning him that should the English Gentleman be also going to Varenna on the same boat, he must be sure to reach Lord Walpole first and warn him.

Everything was now ready for a stealthy departure; the packing had been accomplished so quickly that five minutes only had elapsed since the arrival of the carriage. In silence Suzie and Job came downstairs to the door, wearing cloaks, bonnets, and heavy veiling. As they stood for an instant under the lantern near the carriage, as if waiting to enter it, Gladstone noted a figure wrapped in a cloak which he seemed to recognize 'as that of Susan'. At the same moment Santi, looking about him as though to make sure no one was on the watch, observed the lamp over the door. He cursed Trincavelli for having lighted it and bade him put it out. Without taking leave of Trincavelli, and in total silence, the two women climbed into the carriage while Santi got up behind. As the carriage passed through the gates, Gladstone, standing on tiptoe ('he raised himself up a little'), attempted to see inside, but the blinds were down. He had not dared to go into the courtyard at the moment of departure to satisfy himself of the identity of the heavily veiled woman, for 'weighing all things, and putting all things together, and the extreme undesirableness, from what I believed of the state of Lady Lincoln, of my appearing suddenly before her, I desisted'. The carriage drove towards Lecco on the road to Verona, while Gladstone, exhausted from shock and distress, wrote to his wife.

'Oh my Cathie, I am sorely cast down & sick at heart in this other earthly paradise to which people come for deeds of hell. I am not certain – I may be wrong. Mrs Laurence & Lady Lincoln may be different persons – there are points in which the descriptions are not complete and clear. I have no *demonstration* either of eye or ear – but alas! of *this* there is no doubt whatever, the Mrs Laurence as she is called who refused two times over to see or communicate with me except by verbal message today, & who drove off from her Villa between nine & ten tonight with closed blinds, is *far gone in pregnancy!* It is heartbreaking: but with what joy shall I go down on my knees before her to ask her pardon if, what an if, Mrs Laurence is not Lady L. I do not know how I ought to feel under the great shock of seeming discovery of this terrible calamity. There may be hopes it is a dream.'

Too tired to write more he could yet grieve for the 'triumph of hellish wickedness over a woman of the rarest gifts, and the utter devastation of heart & home & profanation of the holy mystery of marriage. Lord have mercy upon us, Christ have mercy upon us, Lord have mercy upon us.'

Richard Terrell

THE CHIEF JUSTICE
A PORTRAIT FROM THE RAJ

❧

Between 1928 and 1938 Sir Courtney Terrell served as Chief Justice of the Indian provinces of Bihar and Orissa. The appointment, like the man, was unusual in that he had no previous experience of the country – only a strong instinct that he somehow belonged there and, in the event, a remarkable affinity with the Indians themselves. His appointment was a surprise.

Judicial appointments, including the most senior ones, were normally filled by the promotion of men who had served wholly within the provincial field, from the magistracy and the administration. My father's case, however, was most exceptional, for he was sent out directly to his appointment from the Bar in London, at the age of forty-seven, with no previous judicial or official experience at all, even in Britain. He was thus an outsider, an interloper, selected for the job by Lord Birkenhead, the Secretary of State, for his personal qualities, to put strength into an important Indian judicature which had sunk into a condition of serious weakness.

His demeanour was a surprise.

His appearance and the sound of his voice were arresting, partly because of a contradiction between them that one finds sometimes among successful teachers and lecturers. Simple Indians who caught sight of him for the first time in his court were initially frightened. As soon as he spoke the impression melted into gentleness, for his voice was unexpectedly tender, his smile generous, his laughter an explosion of geniality. A frequent use of superlatives in his letters, sometimes exaggerating the emphasis he wished to place on a word, was characteristic of an inner wish to speak, not to write. People who think in the imagery of printed sentences tend to speak with less emphasis than speech actually requires,. Those who imagine continually the sound of their own voices, as Courtney did, tend to overstress in writing what they wish to convey.

His domestic situation was a surprise.

His temperament, attitudes, aspirations, personal and social values, even his pursuits, were coloured by certain oddities in the lives of his grandfather and father during the previous century. Both made unhappy marriages in their twenties, both engaged lustfully in haphazard womanising and both, in their forties, became passionately involved with a mistress. Each of these mistresses produced a large second family of Terrells before formalising the relationship after the death of the senior wife (the African phrase is right, even for Ladbroke Square, London, the scene of many of these happenings). Courtney, in his turn, complicated the precedents by taking as his mistress my mother's elder sister. She, living in a period of somewhat different frustrations, produced no children for him. Instead, she gave him ineffable consolation in the exotic world of his Indian mission. Incidentally, my own affection for her, greater than that for my mother, and my understanding of his predicament was, I am sure, of special importance for this book. But for my sympathy I should not have been the main recipient of his letters in England.

Richard Terrell's portrait, shaped around Sir Courtney's letters, is a sensitive account of a father-son relationship and an insidiously effective re-creation of a very extraordinary man. Iris Portal, in her day a good judge of such things, cited it in a review as 'one of the best books to have come out of the Raj'; and it came with the warmest recommendation – both for its interest and its literary quality – from Paul Scott, himself belatedly acclaimed with the success of the Raj Quartet.

He felt that the coldness, the indifference, even the ostracism of conventional society would destroy him unless he stood up and defied it, asserted his own ego and thrust the world aside. In all his eccentricities, his keen pursuits and enthusiasms, there was a defiant gesture, adamant, brave and extraordinarily thorough. Few who encountered him, in England or in India, did not experience an awareness of something a bit larger than life size ...

His eccentricity showed not in his choice of pursuits but in the technical mastery he brought to them. The most enduring, in which he was active from his early twenties until he went to India and later, was walking. This was something of deep significance in his life ... On his walking tours he wore special, somewhat conspicuous garments: a pale green gaberdine wind jacket with big pockets to hold the one-inch map, a book and an oil-filled compass of military type; handmade crepe-soled shoes and a special gaberdine cap with flaps for the ears in case of rain. He carried a rucksack with a very light frame of cane made in Indonesia, a walking stick and, when the distance to be covered was not great, an expensive-looking camera and folding tripod. In the rucksack were pyjamas and toothbrush, a clean shirt, an aluminium container with half a cold chicken, brown bread and butter, Stilton cheese, an apple and half a bottle of Burgundy. There was a corkscrew and a peculiar aluminium cup which pulled out like a telescope. As for literature, this might include Borrow, Wells, Arnold Bennett or Somerset Maugham and poems by Browning, Kipling or Noyes.

In his relationship with children he was extremely popular and forthcoming. Children of between four years and puberty at once surrendered themselves to him, responding with an abandon which no adult, man or woman, could achieve with him. His love of children was a manifestation of his solitude, and this is very noticeable in his letters. The Indian children of his compound were, for him, like the grandchildren far away.

The courts did not sit every day and there was a great deal to be done. It suited his temperament to be in a position to get the Public Works Department to carry out all the necessary decorations and repairs to the house without having to consult my mother or aunt, whose tastes in such matters he would, in any case, never have felt the slightest obligation to consider. They never criticised this attitude, for it had always been a feature of their landscape, like a range of mountains. Everything, as at our Cornish home, would be done exactly according to his plans, or, rather, his instant decisions. In the same spirit he engaged rapidly a large gathering of servants. He stuck faithfully to nearly all these people for the whole of his ten years in India. Most of the servants brought their wives, babies and young children with them and the whole force numbered over thirty strong, all accommodated in single-storey hutments within the compound at Chhaju Bagh. These people became my father's extended family. Most of them were of very low caste, with many untouchables, and he grew to love them more than any other people in the province. Several of the children he sent to a mission school in Patna, paying the fees out of his salary but arranging with Mr Brown [his private secretary] and the school authorities that no publicity should be given to the matter.

By temperament he knew, inwardly, that he was not a judicial figure at all, whatever the merit of his decisions on the bench. He felt himself to be a demonstrative teacher of other human beings but without the detachment of academic reserve. He felt the empathy of a tragic or comic actor, provided that his part was that of the dominant actor in the play. He yearned for power but derided every party. Persistence in these contradictions in his Indian world, where every action was conspicuous, demanded of him immense personal discipline which he displayed throughout the Indian phase.

If India, since the beginning of British authority, had been subjected to the domination of people like Courtney, instead of the very different kinds of people described in Philip Woodruff's *The Men Who Ruled India*, the country would have become a somewhat different place. Such an imaginary oligarchy would, no doubt, have been massacred to a man, though my father would not have felt any certainty about that. In practice the attitude of British persons with political, official or military responsibility for the government and administration of India had, for generations, expressed itself in two opposite and mutually balancing ways. The possession of power justified its use in the suppression of conduct felt to be repugnant to European values. This was neatly expressed by General Charles Napier who, in Sind in the middle of the nineteenth century, set about the eradication of suttee. A deputation of Brahmins protested to him that he was interfering with local custom. Napier said to them: 'My nation also has a custom. When men burn women alive, we hang them ... Let us all act according to our national customs.' The other, opposite, way was for the British to recognise the limitations of such power as they possessed to interfere with beliefs and practices felt to be wrong. This negative attitude was not initially liberal. British people, since they first set foot in the country, saw everywhere features of Indian existence which they felt to be utterly abominable – sufferings, poverty and cruelty on a scale far surpassing anything conceivable in time of peace in any other part of the world. These evils seemed so powerfully rooted in Indian life, thought and philosophy as to be ineradicable by any effort, any policy whatever, on the part of a handful of British officials, traders and soldiers. This recognition of one's own powerlessness, as well as the utilisation of one's power, was entirely pragmatic. It was the foundation of what, in Nigeria, Lugard was to dignify by the term 'indirect rule', which had long before prevailed in India as common sense. It was not only with the first whispers of the wind of change, the first sentimentality, that the toleration of evil came to be identified with liberal spirit, valued in itself and rationalised in the faraway principle that 'good' government is no substitute for 'self' government. In the minds of those who were not liberals the wind of change was also no more than common sense.

My father viewed the British responsibility in India as a pragmatist and, as such, would no doubt have relished Napier's retort to the Brahmins. In that first hot weather, and thus equipped, he began to work out his policy. As a teacher, he would teach. As an actor, he would act. Having power, he would use it. Knowing the limits of that power he would respect them, or make a show of doing so. Anyway, he would make a show.

If he was to teach he must know his students, enter into their minds. Within a few days of his arrival in Patna he engaged a man to teach him to speak, read and write Urdu and to use both the Persian and the Davanagri scripts. Every day, for half an hour, he sat down on the verandah with his teacher and, within a year, he was able to listen to witnesses and cross-examine them in court, in their own tongue. He could also read vernacular newspapers and talk, not only with his servants, but with colleagues. His discipline in this gradually earned him the respect of Indians he craved to know and to influence.

About the end of March [1938] he became ill one morning as he was about to leave the house for the courts. He went back to bed. With intermittent abdominal pain and vomiting he became helpless. The local doctors decided not to operate again themselves but advised that he be taken at once to London, to the Middlesex Hospital, where facilities for an exploratory operation were available. In mid-April he was taken by special rail coach to Calcutta and put aboard the SS *Strathmore,* bound for Southampton. He spent the voyage in the sick bay ...

My sister, brother and I met the boat train at Waterloo station and travelled in the ambulance to the hospital. We had no notion of the gravity of his condition. He was a young father whose large, strong face upon the pillow in the ambulance showed no sign of illness.

We waited at the hospital whilst he was carried to his bed in a private room – then entered for a few minutes. Sitting up in bed he appeared to adopt a detached judicial posture, raising the palm of his right hand in a familiar, didactic manner, as though he were speaking to a jury: 'Unless we know the evidence of the surgeons we must make up our minds to suspend our opinions entirely. We can only wait and see.' We smiled at him and left.

The operation took place early the next morning. I was not at once informed of the result but was permitted for a few minutes to see him alone. He was calm, able to smile and to speak softly ...

The nurse quietly asked me to leave. I returned to his room a little later. Before entering I saw the surgeon, who happened to be an old friend of my father's, a fellow student with him at the turn of the century. He said the operation had revealed that the abdominal cavity had become so cancerous that no further surgery was possible. I entered the room. He was unconscious, the eyes closed, the chest heaving, the mouth open, dry, gasping.

He died a little later. I did not wait to hear the gasping cease ...

In a little while, like a heavy curtain in the theatre of my father's world, war descended upon the scenes depicted in his letters. When the curtain rose it was not upon the stage of his prediction, nor upon any other visions of the dead.

W. A. Tilney

COLONEL STANDFAST
THE MEMOIRS OF W. A. TILNEY 1868–1947

edited by Nini Murray-Philipson

❧

I had considerable reservations about this book. It seemed at first glance an artlessly written series of extraordinary escapades infused with religious conviction – a sort of G. A. Henty meets Moral Rearmament. It was full, too, of the sporting enthusiasms and social sunshine of class and period – the author saw Queen Mary as his 'guardian angel', which made my toque wobble a little. But the more I looked at it the more I had to admit that there was something really rather winning about it. The author was a brave and decent man – perhaps, as I wrote in the blurb, 'not one you'd want to insure, but then he firmly believed that God was protecting him.' So, with Nini Murray-Philipson's approval (Tilney was her grandfather), I expressed my lingering reservations on the jacket flap and finally urged the reader: 'Don't underestimate the Colonel.' The 'Spectator' reviewer applauded the novelty of a publisher introducing a note of truth into a jacket blurb about what might be wrong with the book and went on to endorse everything that readers have so much liked. So the Colonel has had the last laugh.

Tilney was a cavalryman in the 17th Lancers, served throughout the Boer War, then in India, briefly in the trenches, and then in Ireland in the Troubles. Orphaned at the age of sixteen, he was sent after school to Townsend's, 'a rowdy Army crammer's establishment'.

My guardian and trustees decided to send me to France during the summer holidays to learn French at Châlons-sur-Marne. Pasteur

Andraunt had six pupils, all cramming for the Army, and also a very pretty wife. The poor little man could keep no sort of discipline and allowed us to do anything we liked.

Cecil Noel, of Catmos, Oakham, and I had a dog cart in which we drove a tandem, much to the surprise and annoyance of the Frenchmen, for we used to gallop down the boulevards making terrific blasts on a coaching horn. This was eventually stopped by the authorities – after we had been fined several times. One day we were driving the tandem gently along the boulevard, when we espied Mme Andraunt walking arm in arm with a French officer, a big swell wearing red breeches and decorated with the Légion d'Honneur. They were coming towards us and Cecil Noel said, 'I'll bet you a fiver you don't hit Madame's lover with a plum', at the same time handing me a bag of large blue plums.

I took the bet and hit the man full in the face. He proved to be Major Rabot of the French Cavalry. Two days afterwards three French officers appeared at Andraunt's establishment and presented me with a challenge which I had to accept. I didn't know anything about swords or firearms, nor did we understand who had the choice of weapons, so a friend of mine named Lukis (who became a general in the British Army afterwards) was deputed to find this out. The answer was swords! So I at once repaired to the Maître d'Escrime and never worked so hard at anything in my life.

Almost three days before the duel was due to have taken place I was arrested and taken to the railway station with a ticket to London. Andraunt was in tears, his Mme almost in hysterics. There was such confusion that Andraunt forgot to give me my money for food on the journey. I had about ten francs in my pocket and landed at Charing Cross penniless, about dusk at the end of August.

Before his Boer War adventures he was attached to the aeronautical section of the Royal Engineers at Aldershot, pioneering with balloons.

The CO of the Balloon Section was Colonel Templer, an extraordinary man in many senses; in his way a genius, for he was the inventor of the goldbeater's skin envelope for balloons ... Nothing at that time was known about 'the air' so it was laid down that to get a certificate as a balloonist you had to learn all about the construction of a balloon, make thirty ascents, and take charge of three 'free runs', i.e. in a loose balloon. ...

The first 'free run' I had with Gerry Heath, RE, almost ended in our deaths. It was an ideal day with a light breeze that took us towards Portsmouth from Aldershot. When we neared the sea, Heath ordered me (I was in the net) to pull the valve cord to make our descent, which I did, but instead of coming down we went up to 3,000 feet and, as it was hazy, out of sight of the earth. The next orders I got were in quick succession – to pull the ripping rope; then (in headlong descent) throw overboard everything we could lay our hands on, including our boots ... One did not realise the rapidity of our fall until looking downwards I saw a shining spot in a green park and then felt a terrible crash combined with a miasmal stench of manure.

When I temporarily gained consciousness I found myself in bed with a doctor and two ladies standing alongside it. The place was Rowlands Castle owned by Mr Christie (the hatter). It appeared that when we got into the whirlwind and Heath ordered me to pull the ripping rope, we had fallen like a stone. The shining thing I saw was the butler's bald pate, and we providentially ricocheted off a tree into the manure pit, which saved our lives. Heath had got off with a few bruises and scratches ...

The next free run was pleasant enough and very beautiful as the wind took us up a great part of the Thames Valley. We landed near Swindon. This made me quite keen on free running and I tried to go whenever possible and did twelve free runs in all and only had one further mishap.

Now that I was a qualified aeronaut, Templer ordered me to take a new man for a short free run. When the mouth of the Thames was visible I looked out for a landing place. I put out the anchor in some flats near Tilbury, but unfortunately caught the roof of a shed, which was torn off and the next thing hooked was an outside closet with a woman occupant. She must have had the surprise of her life, as she with the closet was lifted some feet before the anchor gave way and she was dropped in the mud alongside the river.

As the escape valve had been open for the descent we had no lift. Just missing Tilbury Fort we landed on some mud flats – the tide being out – on the other side of the Fort and about half a mile from land. I made signals of distress in hope I might be rescued by a punt when the tide came in. Soon two men came from the shore skating on the mud with mud skates and told me that we would have to wait for an hour before being rescued. When a light punt came down the river I had sunk in the stinking mud up to my waist. We were landed at a margarine factory, given a change of clothes by the foreman and went to London by train from Tilbury. I had arranged for the salvage of the balloon with the foreman of the factory and reported this misadventure at Aldershot the next morning. I imagined that old Templer would be pleased at my escape but to my surprise he was furious and said I should have waited to rescue the balloon and bring it back to Aldershot. He berated me as an unworthy balloonist and sent me off to bring everything back. Now, although there was no code of laws regarding aeronautics in those early days, I felt certain that the lady who had been hooked from the commode and deposited in the Thames mud would make herself nasty on my return. I therefore asked Templer for a party of men to accompany me: thereabouts the wharfingers and bargees are a rough crowd. I had not heard if the woman had suffered any injury. Templer having stipulated that I should defray all expenses, I arrived with three men at the margarine works. Soon a somewhat hostile crowd assembled. They would not permit us to pack up the balloon until I had been confronted by the woman. I was taken to the scene of the accident. She certainly weighed a good fourteen stone, a real good sort, the wife of a fisherman, and treated the incident as a great joke, saying 'If I had not been a bit stout, I might have been taken to heaven, like Elijah!'

The crowd then roared with laughter and when I gave her a fiver she begged me to return as soon as possible and give her a ride in the balloon, saying 'I expect it's more comfortable in that small basket than the ride you gave me on the closet seat.'

Tilney's experiences in Ireland are astonishing. Espousing the cause of loyalist ex-servicemen there at the end of the First World War was a hazardous business, but Tilney somehow survived – indeed a Sinn Fein commander (whom he saved from drowning) told him the Republican Army referred to him as the man they couldn't kill. 'He was much impressed when I told him of my previous escapes and said that it was wonderful that God obviously protected those who put their trust in Him.'

This is the way a cavalryman should deploy his Harley-Davidson in a tight corner.

At every moment I expected to be stopped by a patrol, miss the direction or have a mishap with the bike. It was my first experience of bolting for my life and most harassing to the nerves ...

When approaching Shillelagh I was challenged by a Sinn Fein patrol who barred my path. Pulling my hat well over my face, I charged the two men who stood with rifles advanced on either side of the road. Luckily at this point the road was dead straight, and the day just dawning so that one could see 100 yards ahead. I made straight for the man on the right, a much smaller individual than the one to my left; he was holding his rifle at the advance in a half right direction. Having done so much fighting on horseback, I directed my line of attack towards his right shoulder. The impact was terrific and I thought for a moment I was over, but the sidecar on my left saved an upset and the man seemed to fly yards: the big man on the left was so surprised that he forgot to fire. I reached Tullow without further adventures.

There is an almost joke Irishness about this final extract.

On my return to the Curragh, Sylvester the bookie, reputed to be the cleverest dry fly fisherman in Ireland, suggested that I should come to fish some water he had leased in King's County. I was to provide the lunch and he the motor to take us there. He asked if two jockeys, Beary and Fraser, might also come as his guests, to which proposal I naturally assented. Starting very early we motored a good fifty miles, reaching a beautiful trout stream about 10 a.m. Sylvester told us how lucky he had been to get this fishing on lease for two years at the ridiculously low rent of £20 for the season, as it was one of the best trout streams in Southern Ireland. Sylvester was a loyalist at the Curragh and an ardent Sinn Feiner among his countrymen, so he gave a most amusing descriptions of military doings at the Curragh and Dublin to those rebels whom we met on the way ...

On our arrival at the river, he asked me to fish above the bridge in the morning while he took the two jockeys below and we would all meet at the bridge for lunch. I had an excellent morning's sport, but the sun came out very strongly and I had to take shelter under the shade of the bridge. While waiting for Sylvester's return for lunch I had a snooze.

I was awakened by voices overhead and could not help hearing the conversation, which alluded to the favourite in the Irish Derby which was to be run in about three weeks' time. Sylvester, who was representing a syndicate of bookies, was arranging the race with the two jockeys – a rank outsider was to be allowed to win. Immediately I realised the purport of the conversation I shouted, 'Is that you, Sylvester? Let's have our lunch', and appeared from under the bridge. They were surprised and crestfallen. Towards the end of lunch Sylvester remarked, 'Did ye hear us having a conversation about the Derby?' When I told them I could not help hearing every word, they asked me on my honour not to mention to a soul what I had heard. I laughingly replied that I had given up all interest in racing many years ago, since I could not afford to keep bookmakers.

In the afternoon I fished the lower water and they the upper. Before starting Sylvester explained that his water extended to a part of the river some two miles below. I was busy disgorging a fish on the bank when someone behind said, 'What the hell do you mean by fishing my water without leave? What is your name?' Looking up I recognised an Irish gentleman called Denny, whom I had known years before. I explained that Sylvester had invited me to fish his water and that he and two friends were fishing above the bridge.

'Well, I'm damned,' was all Denny said, and asked me to come with him to find Sylvester, whom we soon came across with his basket full of beautiful trout.

Sylvester's first words were: 'Ah, Mr Denny, I was just after coming down to tell you we are having great sport. When you asked me at the races to have a day on your water, you said I might bring a friend, so I brought the Colonel and we have had a splendid day. Will you have some of the fish?' Denny was speechless, but drew me aside to ask who Sylvester was and how I had made his acquaintance. He had never seen or heard of the man in his life! I told him Sylvester was a well-known bookie at the Curragh and one of the best dry fly fishermen in Ireland. When we rejoined the party, Denny asked him how he managed to catch such a splendid basket of fish. He showed us something I had never heard of before – how every fly, especially may flies, sedges and spinners, changed its hue every hour of the day. His knowledge of insect life seemed quite uncanny, for he showed us how a fish would not look at a female March brown, but speedily swallow a male. Denny told me he had never seen anything like as good a basket of fish as Sylvester caught, and was so pleased that he asked us all down to tea.

This meant whiskey, which was at this time very hard to get in the country and sixteen to eighteen shillings per bottle. As Denny was a keen racing man and had a horse in the Irish Derby, the conversation soon turned to that race and my companion assured him that Golden (the horse that they had arranged should not win) was an absolute certainty. They were brimful of whiskey when we started on our homeward journey. Sylvester the driver was very garrulous, and the others sleepy. We had not gone more that ten or so miles when there was a tremendous bump and the car flew into the air, up a bank on the driver's side, and overturned in a ditch. We had run into a donkey lying in the road.

It was now almost dark. We were at least twenty miles from our destination, the Curragh, with the car hopelessly smashed up. Sylvester instructed the two jockeys to commandeer another car. When they had started on their errand, I remarked that I would pay for the hire of a car to take us home. He replied: 'Devil a bit of it, we officers of the Sinn Fein army have authority to commandeer any car, and we only brought you so that we shouldn't have any trouble with you bloody English.'

In a short time a nice saloon, driven by a chauffeur, pulled up – evidently a squire's property, yet whose car it was I could not ascertain since my companions addressed one another in Gaelic and did not speak a word of English until we had reached the first guard-room of the Curragh, where I was requested to get the car passed through the lines.

Prior to the running of the Irish Derby I did everything in my power to dissuade my friends and brother officers from backing Golden, but the 12th Lancers were obdurate, one officer plonking his all on the horse. A week before the race I had insisted on Sylvester advising Denny that his 'certain winner' tip would not materialise. As I explained, it was too bad first of all to poach his water and then cause him to lose a packet of money.

When the horse arrived at the tape, the jockey reined it back a yard so that when the tape went up the horse's spring was disunited. Unless we had heard that the horse was not going to be allowed to win, few people would understand how Golden got such a bad start, for it lost two lengths then and finished fourth. I went to the start when the race took place and have never seen an example of more consummate horsemanship than Golden's jockey displayed. I had the satisfaction of seeing Denny at the Curragh races and he had not backed Golden.

Cornélie de Wassenaer

A VISIT TO ST PETERSBURG 1824–1825

translated (from the French) and edited by
Igor Vinogradoff

❧

Cornélie de Wassenaer, educated and observant, and the greatest Dutch heiress of her day, went to Russia as maid of honour to the Princess of Orange-Nassau, youngest sister of Emperor Alexander I. The royal party arrived in St Petersburg in November 1824, when Cornélie was twenty-five, and stayed with the Imperial family until the following July. Her journal is wry and perceptive, and as one reviewer wrote, Igor Vinogradoff's 'translation from the original French and the editing are accomplished with a wonderfully erudite ease'. Igor died in 1987 and Dr John Simmons, then Librarian at All Souls, Oxford, helped me over the final editorial lap and did the index.

The Dutch travellers went to Russia by way of Weimar to visit the Princess's sister, the Grand Duchess Maria Pavlovna, before crossing into Russia, where – en route to St Petersburg – they first stayed at the palace at Gatchina as guests of the Dowager Empress Maria Fedorovna, Alexander's mother.

Saturday, October 16th [1824]. It had been fixed in advance for the Princess of Orange to receive people coming to pay court to her. Having put on round dresses without trains we went to the Princess's at a quarter past two. We found Countess Musin-Pushkin already in the antechamber. She is an ugly old person, a lady-in-waiting to the Empress. Countess Litta, the Mistress of the Robes, soon arrived as well. She was to make the presentations – an aged woman too, but with a pleasant appearance. All these women whom etiquette obliges one to embrace are so plastered with powder that one can only kiss them on the chin if one is to avoid a mark. Countess Litta and her husband, the Grand Chamberlain, are Croesuses of wealth. They have a granddaughter, Countess Julia Pahlen, also immensely rich, who is going to unite her fortune with that of Count Samoilov, a young man of rather pleasing appearance. We had all these people to dinner. I was seated one place away from Countess Pahlen, who was wearing a sea-green cashmere shawl, a magnificent present from her fiancé which had cost 20,000 roubles. She had two bracelets on her arms, one with a portrait of Count Samoilov done as an antique bust, the other very simple with a little lock to which her fiancé keeps the key. He had not accompanied his betrothed to Gatchina but the Empress had told her to make him come the next day. The result was that she wrote him a three-page note in pencil on her knee while dinner was in progress and could not rest until they had brought her sealing wax to seal it and ink to write the address. Countess Pahlen's face is quite pretty and she has fine brown eyes, but there is something languid about her which is irritating.

Sunday, October 17th [1824]. We all accompanied the Princess to the Russian service, so as to please the Dowager Empress who likes to go when there is no other church to attend. In the country you can go in muslin or a high silk dress wearing a hat or bonnet. The chapel is in the right wing of the palace, and serves as a passage for everyone on their way there from the main palace block. You try to lean against the wall as much as possible because you dare not sit in a Greek church ... Though this was not the most suitable moment, I could not help staring with amazement at the thin waists of the officers of the Empress's regiment who stood against a window and looked so transparent that you could have cut them in half like wasps. All Russian officers are so terribly tight-laced that they can hardly sit down. Apart from the shell jacket and the belt which had to be pulled tight by two men, so I was told by an officer himself, they wear skin-tight breeches down to their high boots, which makes it impossible for them to bend their knees. Not only officers but ordinary troopers are tight-laced in this way, which inevitably causes aneurisms or other complaints. The Imperial family is no exception. From early youth the cadets are laced like this in the various schools, which makes their chests stick out as though they were stuffed. This unnatural state of things makes them die before their time and it is very rare for a Russian soldier to finish his period of service, supposed to last twenty-five years irrespective of the age at which he enrolled.

After the service we all went home. It was snowing so there was no walk. The Princess was to receive more people before dinner and she advised us to dress our best and above all to wear diamonds; it is the only thing that makes an impression here, because most people have so many and even the young girls are covered with them. Not one of the dresses was particularly tasteful or elegant. Countess Litta presented everyone as she had done the day before. There were more people and the party at dinner was very large. Count Samoilov, Countess Pahlen's fiancé, was there; he is a fine young man but wears spectacles. Unfortunately his future bride seems much more in love than he. In the evening the Dowager Empress appeared at the Arsenal and herself began to read aloud Walter Scott's new novel 'Redgauntlet'. When she was tired she handed the book to General Chernyshev. The reading was only half audible to many of the company. On the following evenings it was continued by Prince Gagarin, who bellowed it out at the top of his voice, and by M. Villamov, the Empress's secretary.

'Redgauntlet' was published in England in 1824, so this French edition must have been produced quite smartly.

The party arrived in St Petersburg on 17 November.

In less that four hours we were in St Petersburg. As we drew near the city the road dropped steeply and you hardly noticed the approach. It was when I saw there was a granite sidewalk on both sides of the road that I realised we had arrived. At first we only saw wooden houses and enclosures, all very neatly aligned. Then suddenly, after crossing a granite bridge, we were struck by the beauty of the view, a fine canal between two granite quays and an iron balustrade, wide straight streets with broad sidewalks, and everywhere spacious low houses – a superb panorama. Of course, I could not help feeling a little sad that I was going to spend the winter here. There is something melancholy about the vastness of these wide streets and huge squares; you hardly see any passers-by and they seem lost in space. Finally we reached the great square with the Admiralty, the Winter Palace and the General Staff building with its imposing archway; we could only gaze in admiration. Then we turned into the Millionaya and stopped in front of the Shepelev Palace, next to the Winter Palace.

We were conducted to a very fine apartment which had been allotted to Mama sixty-five steps above the street ... Everything was furnished with great taste and very clean. We dined in Mama's big room and were given a second footman to wait on us. After dinner General Chernyshev was sent by the Emperor to inquire if we were well-housed.

There is an open fireplace in the big room, the only one in our apartment; everything else is heated by enclosed stoves, which are only lit once a day and keep their heat for twenty-four hours. This makes the temperature very pleasant, and the double windows are a great help in shutting out the cold air. Only one pane, called a 'wasistdas', is opened to air the rooms. I think a good many Russians are even afraid of the little air this pane lets in and make do by airing the rooms in their own way; that is to say by scenting them several times a day. Perhaps this is to get rid of the smell of breath, which is not as a rule very sweet here, partly because of the food and the enormous number of sweets they eat, especially at court where the ladies do not merely chew them all through dinner but send plates back to their rooms. The Princess's apartment is magnificent. One of the rooms is hung with silks of Nassau blue with Orange rosettes. The Winter Palace is inhabited by some two to three thousand people.

Almost at once St Petersburg was struck by the famous flood described by Pushkin in his 'Bronze Horseman'. It was later estimated that 2,500–3,000 people died.

Friday, November 19th. This was a sad and memorable day for the city of St Petersburg. About nine o'clock in the morning we suspected nothing. There had been a thaw the day before, the snow had disappeared and there was a lot of wind. Dr Everard [the Belgian doctor] came to see me and told Pauline [d'Oultremont, a fellow maid of honour] the Neva was rising fast and it was a sight worth seeing, as this only happened rarely. He advised her to take the carriage for a drive on the quays. Fortunately she did not feel like a drive and stayed with me at the window to watch the troops entering and leaving the drill hall where they have their parades in winter. The paving stones were wet with rain and there was more and more water. A little pool formed in front of the drill hall and we laughed at the trouble the officers had in getting across it.

The droshkies and waiting carriages had to move as the water kept rising and in the end we realised the river was pouring into the city ... pedestrians were walking in water up to their waists. The sight became more and more frightening and soon the whole of the huge square was nothing but a lake. Then, when there had been no sign of either droshkies or pedestrians for a considerable time, two coaches and four appeared. One of them luckily got into the Millionaya, the other got caught on the submerged sidewalk and the horses, buffeted by the waves and up to their necks in water, had no strength left to pull. The coachman got off his seat to try to get the coach moving, lost his footing and had to cling to a nearby lamppost. He stuck there for a few moments, looking desperate. Someone shouted to him from a window to save himself and the horses, and leave the carriage.

At last he clambered onto the pole to get back into his seat, crossed himself several times and then set about unharnessing the horses with marvellous energy and coolness. He was just in time, for the water was rising so fast that the horses could hardly keep their heads above it. One of them made several leaps to save itself and looked almost as if it were trying to climb onto the coachman's box, but it calmed down. The others stayed quite still and the little postilion, a child of twelve or fourteen like the majority of them in Russia, did not move from his mount and did his best to help the coachman unharness them, which was not at all easy without a knife or any other tool to undo those soaking straps. The little postilion was the first away on his horse, on whose instinct he relied, and it followed the footway very carefully. He was followed by a second horse, then a third, and they managed to reach higher ground on their own. The coachman was the last to leave, riding the fourth horse and clapping his hands together to warm them after working so long in the cold water. The carriage stayed behind bobbing on the waves with the water up to the windows.

It was a fire that Cornélie witnessed the following March.

Monday, March 14th. In the evening the wooden theatre caught fire. It had only lately been transported from Oranienbaum by order of General Miloradovich. Fortunately because of Lent there was no performance there. The theatre was completely burnt down in a matter of hours, and from our windows we could see the flames over the rooftops. They say the spectacle was magnificent, if melancholy, and many people drove along the other side of the Fontanka canal to watch it. In spite of the excessive heat they managed to save the neighbouring buildings and the stores of wood and merchandise nearby. In St Petersburg no one works to put out fires except trained firefighters. They are a large corps drilled like a special army. Among other things they are taught to throw themselves from third or fourth floor windows into blankets which their comrades hold to catch them. Some of them usually die in every fire, for they are disciplined to take all risks. In this fire three of them disappeared without a trace, but no one mentioned them and when I spoke of it to someone he replied, 'That is their battle. They go into it like other soldiers into action. We do not talk of it.'

Tuesday, March 15th ... We could not avoid dining with Countess

Protassov, the senior maid of honour, who combines the misfortune of blindness with that of being extremely discontented with her fate, though everyone tries to make things as easy as possible for her. She is revolting in her habits and has earned the nickname 'Lady of the Lake', because, as Pauline says, she cannot contain her sluices and sometimes floods the floor. At eight we went to a charming party at Princess Meshcherskii's, where a Lancer officer, an exquisite composer, let us hear his talented compositions. The dry heat is so great in our rooms that the furniture cracks, my hair stays curled all day and Pauline maintains that we are getting smaller. I am small enough already.

Cornélie finally left St Petersburg on 28 July.

Laurence Whistler

THE INITIALS IN THE HEART

❧

This I reissued as one of my Clocktower paperbacks. It's the account of Laurence Whistler's five-year marriage to the actress Jill Furse, a marriage cut tragically short by her death just after the birth of their second child. 'One of the most moving prose threnodies ever written,' the 'Daily Telegraph' reviewer wrote when it came out in 1964, and some people treasure this book. It's certainly affecting, although here and there it's not quite spare enough for me. It works because of its all-excusing integrity. It has tragic decency. There are pitfalls in making the very private very public: the theme of loss can go uncomfortably treacly in the writing – and suddenly it's 'Love Story' and you're being sick over the author's royalty statements.

And thus we arrived at the end of another 'life', I think the forty-second since I went to soldier. That night we talked on till the candles burnt down each side of the bed – talked of the way we would live, of acting and poetry, of our book on Festivals, of relationships hard and easy, of privacy and loyalty, of unselfishness and belief. All the problems were solved; or they were soluble, in one way or another. It was one o'clock when we turned to sleep, and heard for the last time together the low question of the window-latch, and from beyond, already amplified for the winter, the long whisper of the stream that was still time's audible voice, while time was still kind.

There is a kind of equity in bereavement. The joy lost is the measure of the pain, and the antidote for it. Lose little, need little, and find little. Still the best is the worst is the best. For the having of love must

THE INITIALS
IN THE HEART

LAURENCE WHISTLER

Black background, sepia illustration.

always be worth the losing it, when the loss is by separation, not by decay. The joy we had tasted together ruled out despair and any flavour of resentment towards God or 'fate'. That I never felt. Suicide crossed my mind, but only as every fancy crossed it like thistledown. It was repugnant to her thought for me and the children, and would only put some prodigious, if even then not finally uncloseable, distance between us. I had no choice but to try to be what she would want, her acceptance for my model. I must be what she would be if I had died. There was comfort in that pictured reversal, and the few words she had written from time to time about our separation by death made it more acceptably a part of our life. 'And if it were the other way round ...' 'If I ever had to go on without you ...' 'I know completely there would be no end ...' I treasured them now like the fragments of a lost gospel. But if only we had even once talked of death right through, hers and mine. It was folly not to do this. Like most lovers we evaded the issue because we were happy; and then evaded it because we were not. This was a failure.

Bibliographical Appendix

All books (except 'J. R. Hartley' titles) published by Michael Russell (Publishing) Ltd, unless specified as Compton Russell Ltd. Asterisk denotes out of print as at October 2002.

Baring, Maurice, *Dear Animated Bust: Letters to Lady Juliet Duff, France 1915–1918*, introduction by Margaret FitzHerbert, 175pp, 216x138mm, 0 85955 086 9, 1981.*

Blunt, Wilfrid, *Married to a Single Life: An Autobiography 1901–1938*, 320pp, 86 illus., 216x138mm, 0 85955 100 8, 1983.

——, *Slow on the Feather: Further Autobiography 1938–1959*, xviii + 270pp, 110 illus., 216x138mm, 0 85955 135 0, 1986.

Chatwin, Bruce, and Theroux, Paul, *Patagonia Revisited*, illustrated by Kyffin Williams, 62pp, 6 illus., 178x123mm, 0 85955 099 0, 1985.*

Colville, [Sir] John, *Footprints in Time*, 287pp, 4 illus., 234x156mm, 0 85955 110 5, (reissue) 1984.

Douglas-Home, Jessica, *Once Upon Another Time*, 231pp + 8pp illus., 216x138mm, 0 85955 259 4, 2000.

Douglas Home, William, *Sins of Commission*, 96pp, 216x138mm, 0 85955 115 6, 1985.

Elliott, Nicholas, *Never Judge a Man by His Umbrella*, vi + 201pp + 8pp illus., 234x156mm, 0 85955 182 2, 1991.*

——, *With My Little Eye*, 111pp, 216x138mm, 0 85955 200 4, 1993.*

Elliott, W. A. [Hon Lord], *Esprit de Corps: A Scots Guards Officer on Active Service 1943–1945*, 150pp + 8pp illus., 234x156mm, 0 85955 220 9, 1996*; pbk, 229x156mm, 0 85955 236 5, 1997.

Freccia, Massimo, *The Sounds of Memory*, 192pp, 58 illus., 234x156mm, 0 85955 170 9, 1990.

Glazebrook, Philip, *The Electric Rock Garden*, 184pp, 216x138mm, 0 85955 265 9, 2001.

Hartley, Grizel, ed. P. S. H. Lawrence, *Grizel: Grizel Hartley Remembered*, 215pp + 32pp illus., frontis., 234x156mm, 0 85955 181 4, 1991.*

'Hartley, J. R.', *Fly Fishing by J. R. Hartley*, illustrated by Patrick Benson, 127pp, 16 illus., 216x138mm, 0 09 175192 6, Stanley Paul (Random House), 1991.*

——, *J. R. Hartley Casts Again*, illustrated by Patrick Benson, 127pp, 15 illus., 216x138mm, 0 09 177437 3, Stanley Paul (Random House), 1992.*

——, *Golfing by J. R. Hartley*, illustrated by Patrick Benson, 127pp, 16 illus., 216x138mm, Hodder & Stoughton, 1995*; Coronet pbk, 0 340 64451 1, 1996.*

Hinks, Roger, ed. John Goldsmith, *The Gymnasium of the Mind: The Journals of Roger Hinks 1933–1963*, foreword by Kenneth [Lord] Clark, Portrait Memoir by Patrick Leigh Fermor, 311pp, frontis., 216x138mm, 0 85955 096 6, 1984.*

McManners, [Revd Professor] John, *Fusilier: Recollections and Reflections 1939–1945*, 224pp, 8 illus, 6pp maps, 234x156mm, 0 85955 269 1, 2002.

Macvicar, Neil, *A Heart's Odyssey*, 157pp, frontis., 216x138mm, 0 85955 171 7, 1990.

Magan, [Brigadier] William, *Middle Eastern Approaches: Experiences and Travels of an Intelligence Officer 1939–1948*, 176pp + 8pp illus., 216x138mm, 0 85955 266 7, 2001.

Napier, Priscilla, *A Late Beginner*, 263pp, 7pp illus., 234x153mm, Clocktower pbk, 0 85955 242 x, (reissue) 1998.

Nevill, Guy, *Exotic Groves: A Portrait of Lady Dorothy Nevill*, introduction by Elizabeth Longford, 208pp + 8pp illus., 216x138mm, 0 85955 114 8, 1984.*

Russell, Michael, *see* 'Hartley, J. R.'

Scott-Ellis, Priscilla, ed. [Sir] Raymond Carr, *The Chances of Death: A Diary of the Spanish Civil War*, foreword by Gaenor Heathcoat Amory, xvi + 240pp, frontis., 234x156mm, 0 85955 208 x, 1995.

Shand, [Major] Bruce, *Previous Engagements*, 175pp, frontis., 216x138mm, 0 85955 169 5, 1990.

Skinner, Martyn, *Old Rectory or The Interview*, viii + 107pp, 216x138mm, 0 85955 112 1, (reissue) 1984.

Smiley, Lavinia, *A Nice Clean Plate: Recollections 1919–1931*, 96pp, 23 illus., 236x176mm, 0 85955 082 6, 1981.*

Spitzy, Reinhard, *How We Squandered the Reich*, 392pp + 8pp illus., 234x156mm, 0 85955 233 0, 1997*; 234x153mm, Clocktower pbk, 0 85955 249 7, 1999.

Stark, [Dame] Freya, *Letters*, ed. Lucy Moorehead (vols. 1–6), ed. Caroline Moorehead (vols. 7–8): vol. 1 *The Furnace and the Cup, 1914–30*, 318pp, 234x156mm, 0 85955 012 5, Compton Russell, 1974; vol. 2, *The Open Door 1930–33*, 295pp, 234x156mm, 0 85955 021 4, Compton Russell, 1975; vol. 3, *The Growth of Danger 1935–1939*, 312pp, 234x156mm, 0 85955 038 9, Compton Russell, 1976; vol. 4 *Bridge of the Levant 1940–43*, 316pp, 234x156mm, 0 85955 049 4, 1977; vol. 5, *New Worlds for Old 1943–46*, 320pp, 234x156mm, 0 85955 060 5, 1978; vol. 6, *The Broken Road 1947–52*, 296pp, 234x156mm, 0 85955 081 8, 1981; vol. 7, *Some Talk of Alexander 1952–1959*, 320pp, 234x156mm, 0 85955 088 5, 1982; vol. 8, *Traveller's Epilogue 1960–80*, 336pp, 234x156mm, 0 85955 089 3, 1982.

Stone, Reynolds, and Pritchett, [Sir] V. S., *The Turn of the Years: The Seasons' Course* (selected engravings by Reynolds Stone) and *As Old as the Century* (V. S. Pritchett), introduction by Paul Theroux, 48pp, 25 illus., 178x123mm, 0 85955 085 0, 1982.*

Surtees, Virginia, *A Beckford Inheritance: The Lady Lincoln Scandal*, x + 145pp + 2pp illus., 234x156mm, 0 85955 055 9, 1977*; as *The Lady Lincoln Scandal,* 4pp illus., 234x153mm, Clocktower pbk, 0 85955 260 8, 2000.

Terrell, Richard, *The Chief Justice: A Portrait from the Raj*, introduction by Lord Glendevon, 140pp + 5pp illus., 234x156mm, 0 85955 071 9, 1979.*

Theroux, Paul, *Sailing through China*, illustrated by Patrick Procktor, 64pp, 13 illus., 178x123mm, 0 85955 098 2, 1983.*

——, *see* Chatwin, Bruce.

Tilney, W. A., ed. Nini Murray-Philipson, *Colonel Standfast: The Memoirs of W. A. Tilney 1868–1947*, x + 205pp + 8pp illus., 234x156mm, 0 85955 268 3, 2001.

Wassenaer, Cornélie de, ed. and trans. (from French) by Igor Vinogradoff, *A Visit to St Petersburg 1824–1825*, 159pp, 216x138mm, 0 85955 145 8, 1994.

Whistler, [Sir] Laurence, *The Initials in the Heart*, 256pp, 16 illus., 234x153mm, Clocktower paperback, 0 85955 257 8, (reissue) 2000.